Cap
Travel Guide

WANDER WORDS

Copyright © 2023 Wander Words
All rights reserved.

INTRODUCTION

Welcome to the "Cape Cod Travel Guide," your comprehensive resource for exploring the picturesque region of Cape Cod. Nestled on the eastern coast of Massachusetts, Cape Cod is a captivating destination known for its stunning beaches, charming towns, rich history, and breathtaking natural beauty.

In this guide, we invite you to embark on a journey through Cape Cod's diverse offerings and discover the hidden gems that await you. Whether you're a nature enthusiast, history buff, beach lover, or simply seeking a relaxing escape, Cape Cod has something to offer everyone.

Within these pages, you'll find valuable insights into the history, culture, and geography of Cape Cod, providing you with a deeper understanding of this unique destination. We'll also provide practical information on planning your trip, including the best time to visit, transportation options, accommodation choices, and essential items to pack.

As you explore Cape Cod, we'll take you on a tour of its distinct regions, highlighting the popular towns and villages that dot the landscape. From the iconic Cape Cod National Seashore to historic landmarks, lighthouses, museums, and art galleries, we'll showcase the must-see attractions that make Cape Cod a captivating place to visit.

For outdoor enthusiasts, we'll delve into the various adventures available, including hiking and biking trails, kayaking and canoeing excursions, fishing and boating opportunities, and even the chance to witness majestic whales in their natural habitat.

If you're up for day trips and excursions, we'll guide you to nearby destinations such as Martha's Vineyard, Nantucket Island, Provincetown, Plymouth, New Bedford, and Hyannis, each offering its own unique charm and attractions.

Throughout the year, Cape Cod hosts a plethora of events and festivals, from the famous Cape Cod Baseball League to vibrant summer concerts, food and wine festivals, art and craft fairs, and seasonal celebrations. We'll provide insights into the best events to attend during your visit, ensuring you experience the lively spirit of Cape Cod.

Lastly, our practical information section will equip you with essential tips on safety, local customs, useful phrases, emergency contacts, and a curated list of travel resources and websites to enhance your journey. We hope that this "Cape Cod Travel Guide" will inspire and assist you in planning an unforgettable adventure on Cape Cod. Whether you're a first-time visitor or a seasoned traveler, let the natural beauty, rich history, and warm hospitality of Cape Cod captivate your senses and create lasting memories. Prepare yourself to experience the enchantment and fascination of Cape Cod. Let's embark on this incredible journey together!

DISCLAIMER:

This travel guide provides general information and recommendations to enhance your experience, but circumstances can change rapidly, and the information may not always be up to date. Verify details independently before making final decisions. While efforts have been made for accuracy, we can't guarantee completeness, and factors like seasonal variations and local customs can impact services.

Travel involves inherent risks, so prioritize your safety. Consult authorities, obtain travel insurance, and follow official advisories. We disclaim liability for any damages or inconveniences. Responsibility lies with the traveler to exercise judgment, take precautions, respect local culture, and adhere to regulations. Support local businesses and practice sustainable tourism.

Remember, you are ultimately responsible for your travel decisions. Enjoy your journey and stay safe!

CAPE COD TRAVEL GUIDE

CONTENTS

WELCOME TO CAPE COD..1
   ABOUT CAPE COD.. 3
   GEOGRAPHY AND CLIMATE... 4

PLANNING YOUR TRIP..9
   BEST TIME TO VISIT... 9
   GETTING TO CAPE COD... 11
   TRANSPORTATION OPTIONS... 13
   ACCOMMODATION.. 15
   PACKING ESSENTIALS... 17

CAPE COD OVERVIEW...21
   CAPE COD REGIONS...21
   POPULAR TOWNS AND VILLAGES..23
   MUST-SEE ATTRACTIONS... 26
   OUTDOOR ACTIVITIES... 28
   BEACHES AND COASTAL AREAS.. 31
   WILDLIFE AND NATURE PRESERVES..34

EXPLORING CAPE COD..37
   CAPE COD NATIONAL SEASHORE... 38
   HISTORIC SITES AND LANDMARKS...40
   LIGHTHOUSES OF CAPE COD...42
   MUSEUMS AND ART GALLERIES..45
   SHOPPING AND DINING..48
   ENTERTAINMENT AND NIGHTLIFE..51

OUTDOOR ADVENTURES.. 55
   HIKING AND BIKING TRAILS... 56
   KAYAKING AND CANOEING... 59
   FISHING AND BOATING.. 61
   GOLFING AND TENNIS... 64
   WHALE WATCHING.. 66
   CAMPING AND RV PARKS...69

DAY TRIPS AND EXCURSIONS.. 73

CAPE COD TRAVEL GUIDE

    Martha's Vineyard..73
    Nantucket Island...76
    Provincetown...79
    Plymouth..82
    New Bedford..85
    Hyannis and the Kennedy Legacy....................................87

Events and Festivals..91
    Cape Cod Baseball League...92
    Summer Concerts and Performances..............................94
    Food and Wine Festivals...96
    Art and Craft Fairs..98
    Seasonal Celebrations... 100

Practical Information...103
    Local Customs and Etiquette.. 106
    GPS Coordinates Index..109
    Distance Reference Guide..111

Conclusion.. 115

Welcome to Cape Cod

Step foot onto the sandy shores of Cape Cod, and you'll immediately be embraced by a sense of tranquility and timeless beauty. This enchanting destination, located on the eastern coast of Massachusetts, beckons travelers with its pristine beaches, charming coastal towns, and rich maritime heritage.

Welcome to Cape Cod, a place where rolling dunes meet the sparkling waters of the Atlantic Ocean, where historic lighthouses stand as guardians of the coast, and where a vibrant tapestry of nature, culture, and history awaits your discovery.

We invite you to delve into the heart and soul of Cape Cod. Prepare to be captivated by the region's unique character, as you delve into its fascinating history, vibrant cultural heritage, and awe-inspiring geography. Gain a deeper appreciation for what makes Cape Cod such a beloved and cherished destination.

Join us as we unravel the layers of Cape Cod's captivating allure. From its early Native American settlements to its role in the maritime industry and the artistic inspiration it has provided to countless individuals, Cape Cod holds stories that have shaped its identity and continue to enchant visitors from around the world.

As you journey through these pages, you'll come to understand the different regions that make up Cape Cod, each with its own distinct charm and attractions. Discover the popular towns and villages that line the coast, each offering its unique blend of history, culture, and natural beauty. Uncover the hidden gems and lesser-known spots that add a touch of magic to your Cape Cod experience.

Whether you're seeking a quiet retreat to rejuvenate your soul, an adventure-filled getaway in nature's playground, or an exploration of Cape Cod's captivating history and heritage, you'll find it all within these pages. Let Cape Cod captivate your senses, inspire your imagination, and leave an indelible mark on your heart.

Welcome to Cape Cod, where the charm of coastal living, the embrace of nature, and the warmth of the local community await. Prepare to embark on a remarkable journey through one of America's most beloved and treasured destinations.

About Cape Cod

Nestled along the eastern coast of Massachusetts, Cape Cod is a captivating peninsula that has captured the hearts of visitors for generations. Spanning approximately 65 miles (105 kilometers) from the Cape Cod Canal to the tip of Provincetown, this iconic destination offers a unique blend of natural beauty, historic charm, and a relaxed coastal lifestyle. With its picturesque landscapes, Cape Cod showcases a diverse range of environments. From pristine sandy beaches that stretch for miles to rolling dunes, salt marshes, and lush forests, the peninsula is a haven for outdoor enthusiasts and nature lovers alike. Cape Cod also boasts an impressive array of wildlife, including seals, birds, and marine life, adding to its ecological significance.

The history of Cape Cod is rich and fascinating. It was first inhabited by the Wampanoag Native American tribes who relied on the abundant resources of the land and sea. European settlers arrived in the early 17th century, establishing fishing and whaling communities that would shape the region's identity. Today, remnants of Cape Cod's maritime heritage can be seen in its historic lighthouses, maritime museums, and quaint seaside villages.

The character of Cape Cod is defined by its charming towns and villages, each with its own distinct personality. From the bustling streets of Hyannis to the artistic enclave of Provincetown, and from the picturesque streets of Chatham to the serene beauty of Wellfleet, every corner of Cape Cod offers a unique experience for visitors.

Cape Cod is also renowned for its cultural and artistic contributions. It has been a source of inspiration for artists, writers, and musicians throughout history, drawing from its scenic landscapes, serene beaches, and vibrant communities. Within the peninsula, you will discover a wealth of art galleries, theaters, and

cultural festivals, allowing visitors to fully embrace the creative spirit that permeates the region.
Whether you're seeking a relaxing beach vacation, an active outdoor adventure, a journey through history, or a taste of the local cuisine and seafood delicacies, Cape Cod offers a wealth of experiences to suit every traveler's interests. With its warm hospitality, quaint bed and breakfasts, and a vibrant local community, Cape Cod invites you to slow down, unwind, and embrace the timeless allure of coastal living.

Geography and Climate

The geography and climate of Cape Cod play a significant role in shaping the unique character of this captivating destination. From its picturesque coastline to its diversc landscapes, Cape Cod offers a remarkable blend of natural beauty and scenic wonders.

Geographically, Cape Cod is a narrow, sandy peninsula that extends into the Atlantic Ocean. It is situated in southeastern Massachusetts and is bounded by Cape Cod Bay to the north and the Nantucket Sound to the south. The peninsula is connected to mainland Massachusetts by the Cape Cod Canal, which separates it from the rest of the state.

One of the defining features of Cape Cod is its stunning coastline. With more than 500 miles (800 kilometers) of shoreline, Cape Cod boasts an impressive array of sandy beaches, dunes, and coastal habitats. From the popular and bustling beaches to hidden and secluded coves, there is a beach to suit every preference. Visitors can bask in the sun, swim in the refreshing waters, or simply take a leisurely stroll along the shore.

Inland, Cape Cod reveals a diverse and captivating landscape. The region is characterized by rolling dunes, salt marshes, ponds, and forests. The Cape Cod National Seashore, spanning 43,500 acres (17,600 hectares), protects a significant portion of the peninsula's natural landscape, providing opportunities for hiking, wildlife spotting, and immersing oneself in the unspoiled beauty of the area.

Cape Cod experiences a maritime climate, influenced by its proximity to the ocean. Summers are typically mild and pleasant, with average temperatures ranging from the 70s°F (20s°C) to the 80s°F (high 20s to low 30s°C). Cooling sea breezes provide relief on hot days. Spring and fall bring milder temperatures, making them ideal seasons for outdoor activities and exploring the region. Winters on Cape Cod are generally cold, with temperatures ranging from the 30s°F (around 0°C) to the 40s°F (single-digit °C), offering a quieter and serene ambiance.

The climate of Cape Cod also contributes to its unique flora and fauna. The region is home to a variety of plant species, including beach grass, pitch pine, and oak trees. The coastal habitats support a diverse range of bird species, and the surrounding waters are frequented by seals, whales, and other marine life. The geography and climate of Cape Cod create a tapestry of natural wonders and breathtaking vistas, offering visitors an abundance of opportunities to immerse themselves in the outdoors. From sandy beaches and rolling dunes to tranquil forests and scenic vistas, Cape Cod's diverse landscapes beckon adventurers and nature enthusiasts alike.

In the following chapters, we will delve deeper into the specific regions, attractions, and outdoor activities that make Cape Cod a paradise for nature lovers and those seeking outdoor adventures. Get ready to explore the remarkable geography and embrace the ever-changing moods of the Cape Cod climate as you embark on your journey through this captivating destination.

CAPE COD TRAVEL GUIDE

Planning Your Trip

Embarking on a journey to Cape Cod is an exciting prospect, filled with anticipation and the promise of unforgettable experiences. To make the most of your time on this captivating peninsula, careful planning and preparation are key.

Timing is crucial when it comes to visiting Cape Cod. The region experiences distinct seasons, each offering its own unique charm. Whether you prefer the vibrant energy of the summer months, the serene beauty of spring and fall, or the peaceful ambiance of winter, understanding the best time to visit Cape Cod will enhance your overall experience.

Best Time to Visit

Determining the best time to visit Cape Cod largely depends on your personal preferences and the experiences you seek. Each season on the peninsula offers its own distinct charm, allowing visitors to tailor their trip to suit their interests.

Summer is the peak tourist season on Cape Cod, spanning from June to August. During these months, the weather is generally warm and sunny, making it perfect for beach lovers and outdoor enthusiasts. The vibrant coastal towns come alive with bustling activity, and the beaches are dotted with sunbathers, swimmers, and surfers. Summer is also the time for various events, festivals, and outdoor concerts, adding to the lively atmosphere. However, it's important to note that summer is also the busiest and most crowded time, so expect larger crowds and higher accommodation prices.

Spring and fall are considered shoulder seasons on Cape Cod, offering milder temperatures and fewer crowds. Spring, from April to May, brings blooming flowers, awakening nature, and the chance to witness the region's natural beauty in full bloom. Fall, from September to October, treats visitors to crisp air, stunning foliage, and a sense of tranquility as the summer crowds disperse. These seasons are ideal for nature walks, scenic drives, and exploring the quaint towns at a more leisurely pace.

Winter, from November to March, offers a different side of Cape Cod. While the temperatures are colder, the peninsula takes on a serene and peaceful ambiance. Winter brings the opportunity for quiet walks on deserted beaches, cozy evenings by the fireplace, and discovering the local charm without the hustle and bustle. Some attractions may have limited hours or closures during this time, but it's a great season for those seeking a tranquil retreat or a unique winter experience.

When planning your trip, it's important to consider your interests, weather preferences, and the kind of experience you desire. Keep in mind that Cape Cod's weather can be unpredictable, so it's advisable to pack layers and be prepared for changes.

No matter the season you choose to visit, Cape Cod's natural beauty and charming coastal towns will leave you enchanted. Whether you prefer the vibrant energy of summer, the tranquility of shoulder seasons, or the serene winter ambiance, Cape Cod welcomes you with its timeless allure and warm hospitality.

Getting to Cape Cod

Getting to Cape Cod is a seamless and enjoyable journey, with various transportation options available to suit your preferences and needs. Whether you're traveling from nearby cities or from afar, reaching this captivating peninsula is a straightforward process.

By Air: If you're arriving from a distant location, the most convenient option is to fly into one of the nearby airports. The closest major airport is Boston Logan International Airport (BOS), located approximately 70 miles (113 kilometers) northwest of Cape Cod. From the airport, you can rent a car, take a taxi, or utilize ground transportation services to reach your desired destination on Cape Cod. Some smaller airports, such as Barnstable Municipal Airport (HYA) in Hyannis, offer regional flights and can be a convenient choice for travelers coming from nearby locations.

By Car: Cape Cod is easily accessible by car via the Cape Cod Canal. If you're driving from Boston or other parts of Massachusetts, you can take Interstate 93 south to Route 3 south, which will lead you to the Sagamore Bridge or the Bourne Bridge, both of which span the Cape Cod Canal. Once on Cape Cod, the scenic Route 6, also known as the Mid-Cape Highway, serves as the main artery connecting the different towns and regions. It's important to note that traffic can be heavy during peak tourist seasons, so planning your travel times accordingly can help avoid congestion.

By Bus: Several bus services operate routes to Cape Cod from various locations. The Plymouth & Brockton Street Railway Company offers regular service from Boston's South Station and Logan Airport to various destinations on Cape Cod. Additionally, other bus companies provide connections to Cape Cod from neighboring states, offering a convenient and cost-effective transportation option for travelers.

By Ferry: Another enchanting way to reach Cape Cod is by ferry. If you're coming from nearby islands or coastal areas, ferries offer a scenic and enjoyable mode of transportation. Ferries operate from locations such as Boston, Plymouth, New Bedford, and Rhode Island, with destinations including Provincetown, Martha's Vineyard, and Nantucket. Ferry schedules and availability may vary depending on the season, so it's advisable to check ahead and make reservations if needed.

Once you've arrived on Cape Cod, various transportation options are available to explore the region. Renting a car provides the most flexibility, allowing you to easily navigate the different towns and attractions. Additionally, taxis, rideshare services, and local public transportation, such as buses and shuttles, are available for convenient travel within Cape Cod.

Planning your transportation to Cape Cod ensures a smooth start to your journey. Whether you choose to fly, drive, take a bus, or hop on a ferry, the peninsula eagerly awaits your arrival, ready to envelop you in its coastal charm and natural beauty.

Transportation Options

Once you have arrived in Cape Cod, it's essential to familiarize yourself with the transportation options available to navigate the region efficiently and make the most of your time on the peninsula. From exploring the scenic coastline to venturing into the charming towns and villages, Cape Cod offers various transportation choices to suit your preferences.

1. **Car Rental:** Renting a car is a popular choice among visitors to Cape Cod. It provides the freedom and flexibility to explore the region at your own pace. Several car rental companies have offices at airports and major towns on the peninsula, allowing you to conveniently pick up and drop off your vehicle. Having a car enables you to easily access the different attractions, beaches, and landmarks scattered throughout Cape Cod.
2. **Taxis and Rideshare Services:** Taxis are readily available in Cape Cod, particularly in popular towns and tourist areas. You can hail a taxi from designated stands or book one in advance. Rideshare services such as Uber and Lyft also operate in the region, offering convenient transportation options for getting around.
3. **Buses and Shuttles:** Cape Cod Regional Transit Authority (CCRTA) operates a comprehensive bus system that connects various towns and villages on the peninsula.

The buses are a convenient and affordable mode of transportation, with regular schedules and routes covering major tourist areas. Additionally, some towns offer free or low-cost shuttle services during peak tourist seasons, making it easier to explore specific areas without worrying about parking or driving.
4. **Bike Rentals:** Cape Cod is known for its scenic bike trails and cycling-friendly environment. Many towns have bike rental shops where you can rent bicycles for a few hours or the entire duration of your stay. Exploring Cape Cod on a bike allows you to appreciate the stunning

Accommodation

Choosing the right accommodation is a crucial aspect of planning your trip to Cape Cod. The peninsula offers a diverse range of options to suit every budget, preference, and travel style. Whether you're seeking luxurious beachfront resorts, cozy bed and breakfasts, or family-friendly vacation rentals, Cape Cod has something to fulfill your needs.
1. **Hotels and Resorts:** Cape Cod is home to a variety of hotels and resorts that cater to different budgets and preferences. From upscale oceanfront resorts with full-service amenities to charming boutique hotels and cozy inns, you'll find a wide range of options throughout the region. Many hotels offer on-site restaurants, pools, spas, and recreational facilities, ensuring a comfortable and enjoyable stay.

2. **Bed and Breakfasts:** Cape Cod is renowned for its charming bed and breakfast establishments. These quaint and intimate accommodations provide a personalized experience, often hosted by friendly innkeepers who offer insights into the local area. Bed and breakfasts are typically located in historic homes or beautifully restored buildings and offer cozy rooms, homemade breakfasts, and a warm ambiance that captures the essence of Cape Cod's hospitality.
3. **Vacation Rentals:** If you're traveling with a group or desire a home-away-from-home experience, vacation rentals are an excellent option. Cape Cod boasts a wide selection of vacation homes, cottages, and condos available for short-term rental. Renting a vacation property allows you to have more space, privacy, and the freedom to create your own schedule. Many vacation rentals are fully equipped with kitchens and amenities, making them ideal for families or those who prefer a self-catering option.
4. **Campgrounds and RV Parks:** For nature enthusiasts and outdoor lovers, Cape Cod offers several campgrounds and RV parks. Whether you prefer tent camping or have your own recreational vehicle, these accommodations provide a unique experience amidst the peninsula's natural beauty. Camping facilities often feature amenities such as picnic areas, playgrounds, and access to trails and beaches.

When choosing your accommodation, consider the location and proximity to the attractions and activities you plan to explore. Cape Cod is divided into distinct regions, each with its own charm and offerings. Popular areas include Provincetown, Hyannis, Chatham, Falmouth, and Wellfleet. Selecting an accommodation that aligns with your preferred region will enhance your overall experience.

It's advisable to make reservations in advance, especially during the peak summer season when accommodations tend to fill up quickly. Research and compare options, read reviews, and consider your budget and preferences to find the perfect place to stay during your visit to Cape Cod.

With its wide array of accommodation choices, Cape Cod ensures that every traveler can find their ideal retreat, allowing you to relax, unwind, and make lasting memories in this captivating coastal paradise.

Packing Essentials

When preparing for your trip to Cape Cod, packing the right essentials ensures you have a comfortable and enjoyable experience on the peninsula. Consider the following items to include in your packing list:

1. **Clothing:** Cape Cod's weather can be variable, so it's wise to pack layers that you can easily add or remove as needed. Include lightweight and breathable clothing for the warm summer months, such as shorts, T-shirts, sundresses, and swimsuits. Don't forget to pack a hat, sunglasses, and sunscreen to protect yourself from the sun's rays. For spring and fall visits, pack a light jacket or sweater for cooler evenings. Winter travelers should pack warm

clothing, including a coat, hat, gloves, and scarves, as temperatures can be chilly.
2. **Footwear:** Comfortable walking shoes are essential for exploring Cape Cod's diverse landscapes. Pack a pair of sneakers or walking shoes for outdoor activities and sightseeing. If you plan to visit the beaches, include flip-flops or sandals for easy beach access. Hiking boots or sturdy shoes are recommended for exploring nature trails and hiking areas.
3. **Beach Essentials:** Cape Cod is renowned for its beautiful beaches, so be sure to pack beach essentials. Include a beach towel, beach mat or chair, and a beach bag to carry your belongings. Don't forget your swimsuit, sunscreen, and a cover-up or light clothing for sun protection. If you enjoy water activities, consider packing snorkeling gear, beach toys, or a beach umbrella for added shade.
4. **Outdoor Gear:** If you plan to engage in outdoor activities such as hiking, biking, or kayaking, pack the necessary gear. This may include a backpack, water bottle, insect repellent, a hat for sun protection, and appropriate equipment for your chosen activities. If you plan to bike, consider bringing your helmet or renting one locally.
5. **Electronics and Accessories:** Don't forget to pack your essential electronics such as your phone, camera, or GoPro to capture memorable moments. Remember to bring charging cables, extra batteries, and a power bank for extended outings. If you have a GPS

device or prefer using your smartphone for navigation, make sure to download offline maps or have access to a reliable navigation app.
6. **Travel Documents:** It's important to carry essential travel documents with you. This includes your identification (such as a driver's license or passport), travel insurance information, flight or transportation tickets, accommodation reservations, and any necessary travel permits or visas.
7. **Other Essentials:** Don't overlook other essentials such as a reusable water bottle, snacks, a small first-aid kit, any necessary medications, and a travel guidebook or maps for reference. It's also a good idea to pack a small umbrella or raincoat, as Cape Cod can experience occasional showers.

Remember to pack according to the season and activities you plan to undertake during your visit. By packing these essential items, you'll be well-prepared for your Cape Cod adventure, ensuring a comfortable and enjoyable experience as you explore the peninsula's natural beauty and charming towns.

Cape Cod Overview

Cape Cod Regions

Cape Cod is a diverse peninsula, comprised of various regions, each offering its own unique character and attractions. Understanding the distinct qualities of these regions will help you plan your itinerary and make the most of your Cape Cod experience. Let's explore the different regions that make up this captivating destination:

1. **Upper Cape:** Located at the westernmost part of Cape Cod, the Upper Cape is where your journey begins as you cross the iconic Bourne or Sagamore Bridge. This region includes towns such as Bourne, Sandwich, Falmouth, and Mashpee. The Upper Cape showcases a blend of natural beauty and rich history, with highlights including the charming Sandwich Village, the Shining Sea Bikeway, and the stunning beaches of Falmouth. Explore the Cape Cod Canal, a man-made waterway that

connects Cape Cod Bay to Buzzards Bay, offering scenic walking and biking paths along its shores.
2. **Mid-Cape:** Stretching across the central part of Cape Cod, the Mid-Cape region encompasses towns like Barnstable, Hyannis, Yarmouth, and Dennis. This area is known for its bustling harbors, vibrant Main Streets, and family-friendly attractions. Discover the maritime heritage of Hyannis and visit the John F. Kennedy Hyannis Museum, which honors the legacy of the former U.S. president. Enjoy the pristine beaches of Dennis and explore the Cape Cod Museum of Art in Dennis Village. Mid-Cape is also a hub for shopping, dining, and entertainment, with a wide array of options to suit every taste.
3. **Lower Cape:** Moving eastward, you'll reach the Lower Cape, a region characterized by its picturesque landscapes, charming villages, and historic landmarks. Towns in this area include Brewster, Harwich, Chatham, and Orleans. The Lower Cape boasts stunning beaches, tranquil ponds, and the Cape Cod National Seashore, a preserved area spanning 40 miles along the outer coastline. Explore the quaint town centers, visit the Cape Cod Museum of Natural History in Brewster, and take in the scenic beauty of Nauset Beach in Orleans.
4. **Outer Cape:** As you continue your journey along the peninsula's easternmost point, you'll reach the Outer Cape, a region renowned for its unspoiled natural beauty and artistic

inspiration. The towns of Eastham, Wellfleet, Truro, and Provincetown make up this area. Explore the Cape Cod National Seashore, which encompasses pristine beaches, towering sand dunes, and picturesque hiking trails. Wellfleet is famous for its oysters, art galleries, and the Wellfleet Harbor Actors Theater. Finally, reach the vibrant and eclectic town of Provincetown, known for its LGBTQ+ culture, art scene, and lively atmosphere.

Each region of Cape Cod offers its own distinct allure, from historical landmarks and scenic beauty to cultural treasures and recreational opportunities. Whether you choose to explore one specific region or embark on a journey across the entire peninsula, you'll find that Cape Cod's diversity ensures there's something for every traveler to discover and appreciate.

Popular Towns and Villages

Cape Cod is dotted with a multitude of towns and villages, each with its own unique charm and character. From historic centers to coastal retreats, these towns and villages are the heart and soul of the peninsula, offering visitors a glimpse into Cape Cod's rich cultural heritage and captivating coastal lifestyle. Let's explore some of the popular towns and villages that you won't want to miss during your Cape Cod adventure:

1. **Provincetown:** Located at the tip of Cape Cod, Provincetown is a vibrant and eclectic town known for its artistic spirit, LGBTQ+ culture, and picturesque beauty. Stroll down

Commercial Street, lined with galleries, boutiques, and restaurants. Visit the Pilgrim Monument and Provincetown Museum, offering breathtaking views of the town and its surroundings. Provincetown is also famous for its stunning beaches, dune trails, and whale watching excursions.

2. **Chatham:** Nestled on the southeastern coast of Cape Cod, Chatham exudes quintessential New England charm. Explore the historic Main Street, lined with charming shops, art galleries, and restaurants. Visit the Chatham Lighthouse, a scenic landmark overlooking the Atlantic Ocean. Chatham is also known for its beautiful beaches, including Lighthouse Beach and Cockle Cove Beach, where you can relax, swim, or catch a spectacular sunset.

3. **Sandwich:** As Cape Cod's oldest town, Sandwich boasts a rich history and a charming village center. Take a step back in time as you explore the Heritage Museums & Gardens, showcasing art, history, and meticulously manicured gardens. Visit the Sandwich Glass Museum, highlighting the town's glassmaking heritage. Enjoy a leisurely stroll along the picturesque Sandwich Boardwalk, which extends over the salt marshes and offers scenic views.

4. **Hyannis:** Located in the town of Barnstable, Hyannis is a bustling hub and a popular destination for visitors to Cape Cod. Discover the Kennedy legacy at the John F. Kennedy Hyannis Museum and explore the bustling

waterfront district with its shops, restaurants, and entertainment venues. Take a scenic harbor cruise or hop on a ferry to explore the nearby islands of Martha's Vineyard and Nantucket.
5. **Wellfleet:** Known for its natural beauty and artistic inspiration, Wellfleet is a haven for nature lovers and art enthusiasts. Explore the picturesque Wellfleet Harbor, where you can enjoy fresh seafood and watch fishing boats come and go. Discover the galleries and studios that showcase the town's vibrant art scene. Don't miss the Wellfleet Bay Wildlife Sanctuary, offering nature trails and opportunities for birdwatching.

These are just a few of the many captivating towns and villages that adorn Cape Cod's landscape. Each destination offers its own unique attractions, whether it's historical landmarks, cultural treasures, natural wonders, or coastal beauty. As you explore the various towns and villages, you'll find that they collectively contribute to the tapestry of Cape Cod, creating an unforgettable experience for every visitor.

Must-See Attractions

Cape Cod is home to a plethora of must-see attractions that showcase the region's natural beauty, rich history, and cultural heritage. From pristine beaches and picturesque lighthouses to captivating museums and charming landmarks, these attractions offer a glimpse into the essence of Cape Cod. Whether you're a nature enthusiast, history buff, or art lover, be sure to include these must-see attractions on your Cape Cod itinerary:

- **Cape Cod National Seashore:** Stretching along 40 miles of the outer coastline, the Cape Cod National Seashore is a pristine and protected area of stunning natural beauty. Explore the scenic beaches, hike the trails through sand dunes and marshes, and admire the breathtaking coastal landscapes. Don't miss iconic spots like Coast Guard Beach, Marconi Beach, and Race Point Beach.
- **Pilgrim Monument and Provincetown Museum:** In Provincetown, ascend the Pilgrim Monument, a towering structure that commemorates the arrival of the Pilgrims in 1620. Enjoy panoramic views of Provincetown and learn about the town's history at the Provincetown Museum located at the monument's base.
- **Cape Cod Museum of Natural History:** Located in Brewster, the Cape Cod Museum of Natural History is a treasure trove of exhibits that showcase the region's diverse ecosystems and wildlife. Explore interactive displays, nature trails, and the butterfly house, and attend educational programs and events that celebrate Cape Cod's natural wonders.
- **Cape Cod Rail Trail:** For outdoor enthusiasts, the Cape Cod Rail Trail offers an opportunity to explore the peninsula's scenic beauty on a bike or on foot. This 22-mile paved trail follows the route of the former Cape Cod railroad, passing through charming towns, wooded areas, and cranberry bogs.

- **Nauset Light:** Located in Eastham, Nauset Light is one of Cape Cod's iconic lighthouses. Admire its picturesque setting and learn about its history as you explore the grounds. The nearby Nauset Light Beach is also a popular spot for sunbathing and beachcombing.
- **Plimoth Patuxet Museums:** While technically located just off Cape Cod in Plymouth, the Plimoth Patuxet Museums are worth a visit to delve into the history of the Pilgrims and the Wampanoag people. Explore the living history exhibits at Plimoth Plantation and learn about the Native American culture at the Wampanoag Homesite.
- **Sandwich Glass Museum:** Visit the Sandwich Glass Museum in the town of Sandwich to learn about the area's glassmaking heritage. Admire exquisite glasswork, watch live demonstrations, and explore the museum's collection of antique glass pieces.
- **Cape Cod Maritime Museum:** Located in Hyannis, the Cape Cod Maritime Museum is dedicated to preserving and promoting Cape Cod's maritime heritage. Explore exhibits that showcase the region's seafaring history, including displays on whaling, fishing, and boatbuilding.

These are just a few of the many must-see attractions that await you on Cape Cod.

Outdoor Activities

Cape Cod's stunning natural landscapes and coastal beauty make it an ideal destination for outdoor enthusiasts. From sandy beaches and scenic trails to water activities and wildlife encounters, the peninsula offers a wide range of outdoor activities to suit every interest and skill level. Embark on a thrilling exploration of Cape Cod's natural beauty with these exciting outdoor activities:

1. **Beach Exploration:** With over 500 miles of coastline, Cape Cod is renowned for its pristine beaches. Spend your days sunbathing, swimming, and beachcombing on the sandy shores. From the popular Coast Guard Beach in Eastham to the tranquil Bank Street Beach in Harwichport, each beach has its own unique charm. Explore the tidal pools, collect seashells, or simply relax and soak up the sun.
2. **Hiking and Nature Trails:** Lace up your hiking boots and embark on an adventure through Cape Cod's scenic trails. The Cape Cod National Seashore offers a network of trails that wind through dunes, marshes, and forests, providing breathtaking views of the coastline. The Atlantic White Cedar Swamp Trail in Wellfleet and the Beech Forest Trail in Provincetown are popular choices for nature enthusiasts. Additionally, the Cape Cod Pathways trails offer a variety of paths that showcase the region's diverse landscapes.
3. **Biking:** Cape Cod's flat terrain and scenic routes make it a cyclist's paradise. Pedal along the Cape Cod Rail Trail, a paved path that

spans from Dennis to Wellfleet, offering beautiful views of forests, cranberry bogs, and charming towns along the way. Enjoy the fresh air and explore the peninsula at your own pace as you pass through picturesque landscapes and quaint villages.
4. **Kayaking and Paddleboarding:** Discover Cape Cod's coastal beauty from a different perspective by kayaking or paddleboarding along its waterways. Rent a kayak or paddleboard and navigate the calm waters of Cape Cod Bay, Nantucket Sound, or the Cape Cod Canal. Paddle through salt marshes, spot wildlife such as seals and shorebirds, and enjoy the serenity of the surrounding nature.
5. **Whale Watching:** Cape Cod is renowned for its whale watching opportunities, offering a chance to observe these majestic creatures in their natural habitat. Hop on a whale watching excursion from Provincetown or Barnstable and venture into the Stellwagen Bank National Marine Sanctuary. Witness the awe-inspiring sight of humpback, finback, and minke whales breaching and spouting as expert naturalists provide educational insights.
6. **Fishing:** Cape Cod's abundant waters make it a prime destination for fishing enthusiasts. Whether you prefer deep-sea fishing, surfcasting from the shore, or fly fishing in freshwater ponds and rivers, there are plenty of opportunities to reel in a variety of fish species, including striped bass, bluefish, and flounder. Charter a fishing boat or simply cast

your line from one of the peninsula's scenic fishing spots.
7. **Golfing:** Cape Cod boasts several championship golf courses that offer breathtaking views and challenging play. Tee off against picturesque backdrops of ocean vistas, rolling dunes, and lush green fairways. Enjoy a round of golf at renowned courses like the Cape Cod National Golf Club in Brewster or the Ocean Edge Resort & Golf Club in Brewster and explore the peninsula's golfing scene.
8. **Birdwatching:** Cape Cod is a haven for birdwatchers, with its diverse habitats attracting a wide range of bird species. Visit the Wellfleet Bay Wildlife Sanctuary or the Monomoy National Wildlife Refuge in Chatham for excellent birdwatching opportunities. Observe migratory birds, shorebirds, ospreys, and other fascinating species in their natural habitats.

Engaging in these outdoor activities allows you to fully embrace and experience the natural splendor of Cape Cod, while indulging in recreational pursuits and creating cherished memories along the way. Whether you seek relaxation, adventure, or a connection with nature, Cape Cod's outdoor offerings are sure to delight visitors of all ages.

Beaches and Coastal Areas

Cape Cod is synonymous with beautiful beaches and picturesque coastal areas. With its expansive coastline, the peninsula offers a diverse range of beach experiences, from serene and secluded spots to

vibrant and bustling shores. Whether you're seeking relaxation, water sports, or scenic beauty, Cape Cod's beaches and coastal areas have something for everyone. Here are some of the must-visit beaches and coastal areas on Cape Cod:
1. **Coast Guard Beach (Eastham):** Located within the Cape Cod National Seashore, Coast Guard Beach is consistently ranked as one of the top beaches in the country. Its pristine sandy shores, picturesque dunes, and breathtaking views of the Atlantic Ocean make it a true gem. Take a stroll along the shoreline, swim in the refreshing waters, or simply relax on the soft sand and soak up the sun.
2. **Nauset Beach (Orleans):** As one of Cape Cod's most iconic and popular beaches, Nauset Beach stretches for miles along the Atlantic coast. Known for its towering sand dunes and stunning vistas, it offers ample space for sunbathing, picnicking, and beachcombing. Enjoy the rolling waves, go for a refreshing swim, or try your hand at surfing.
3. **Mayflower Beach (Dennis):** Mayflower Beach is a family-friendly beach with its calm waters and tidal pools, making it perfect for children to splash and explore. Its wide sandy shoreline provides plenty of space for sunbathing and building sandcastles. Don't miss the breathtaking sunsets that paint the sky with vibrant hues.
4. **Race Point Beach (Provincetown):** Situated at the tip of Cape Cod, Race Point Beach is a haven for nature lovers and adventure seekers.

Its rugged beauty, pristine sand, and panoramic views of the Atlantic Ocean attract visitors year-round. Explore the dunes, go for a refreshing swim, or embark on a scenic hike along the shoreline.

5. **Old Silver Beach (Falmouth):** Known for its powdery white sand and crystal-clear waters, Old Silver Beach is a beloved destination for locals and visitors alike. Its calm and shallow waters make it ideal for swimming and wading, while the expansive beach offers ample space for sunbathing and beach games. Enjoy stunning views of Buzzards Bay and savor the tranquility of this beautiful beach.

6. **Craigville Beach (Barnstable):** Craigville Beach is a popular beach located on Nantucket Sound. With its long sandy stretch, gentle waves, and warm waters, it's a favorite spot for families and sun seekers. Take a leisurely walk along the shoreline, swim in the calm waters, or enjoy a picnic overlooking the scenic beauty of the beach.

7. **Sandy Neck Beach (Barnstable):** Sandy Neck Beach is a picturesque beach that stretches along a barrier beach and marshland. It offers a serene and natural setting, perfect for nature enthusiasts and birdwatchers. Explore the dunes, go for a hike or a scenic off-road drive, and enjoy the tranquility of this beautiful coastal area.

These are just a few examples of the many stunning beaches and coastal areas that Cape Cod has to offer. From serene and secluded coves to lively and family-friendly shores, each beach and coastal area has its own unique charm. Whether you're seeking relaxation, water activities, or simply a place to enjoy the beauty of nature, Cape Cod's beaches and coastal areas are sure to captivate your senses and create lasting memories.

Wildlife and Nature Preserves

Cape Cod is not only renowned for its beautiful beaches and coastal areas but also for its diverse wildlife and nature preserves. The peninsula is home to a variety of ecosystems, including salt marshes, forests, ponds, and dunes, which provide habitats for numerous plant and animal species. Whether you're a nature enthusiast, a birdwatcher, or simply someone who appreciates the wonders of the natural world, Cape Cod's wildlife and nature preserves offer opportunities for exploration and discovery. Here are some remarkable locations where you can fully experience the region's breathtaking natural beauty:

1. **Wellfleet Bay Wildlife Sanctuary (Wellfleet):** Operated by Mass Audubon, the Wellfleet Bay Wildlife Sanctuary encompasses more than 1,000 acres of salt marsh, barrier beach, woodlands, and freshwater ponds. Explore the sanctuary's trails and boardwalks, and discover diverse bird species, including herons, shorebirds, and ospreys. Learn about the unique ecology of Cape Cod through interactive exhibits and educational programs.
2. **Monomoy National Wildlife Refuge (Chatham):** Located on Monomoy Island, the Monomoy National Wildlife Refuge is a haven for migratory birds and marine life. Take a

boat or kayak trip to the refuge and explore its pristine beaches, dunes, and salt marshes. Observe seals, shorebirds, and waterfowl in their natural habitat and enjoy the tranquility of this remote and protected area.
3. **Cape Cod Museum of Natural History (Brewster):** While primarily a museum, the Cape Cod Museum of Natural History also features nature trails and exhibits that highlight the peninsula's natural wonders. Walk along the museum's trails, which wind through salt marshes and uplands, and learn about Cape Cod's diverse ecosystems. Keep an eye out for wildlife, such as turtles, frogs, and various bird species.
4. **Nickerson State Park (Brewster):** Nickerson State Park offers a picturesque setting for outdoor enthusiasts and nature lovers. Explore the park's extensive trail system, which winds through woodlands, kettle ponds, and cranberry bogs. Keep an eye out for wildlife, including deer, foxes, and a variety of bird species. Enjoy activities such as hiking, biking, fishing, and swimming in the park's freshwater ponds.
5. **Mashpee National Wildlife Refuge (Mashpee):** This refuge encompasses a diverse range of habitats, including forests, wetlands, and freshwater ponds. Embark on a nature walk or birdwatching excursion along the refuge's trails, where you may spot migratory birds, turtles, and other wildlife.

The refuge is also home to the endangered New England cottontail rabbit.

6. **Ashumet Holly Wildlife Sanctuary (Falmouth):** Managed by the Thornton W. Burgess Society, the Ashumet Holly Wildlife Sanctuary is a hidden gem for nature enthusiasts. Explore the sanctuary's trails, which wind through woodlands and wetlands, and admire the diverse collection of holly trees. Keep an eye out for resident and migratory bird species, as well as other wildlife that call the sanctuary home.

These wildlife and nature preserves offer visitors a chance to connect with the natural world, observe wildlife in their habitats, and learn about the unique ecosystems that make Cape Cod such a special place. Whether you're interested in birdwatching, hiking, or simply enjoying the serenity of nature, these preserves provide a haven for exploration and appreciation of Cape Cod's natural treasures.

Exploring Cape Cod

Once you've familiarized yourself with the essentials of Cape Cod and have a sense of what the region has to offer, it's time to embark on your journey of exploration. Cape Cod is a place of endless discovery, where each town, village, and landmark holds its own unique charm and allure.

Get ready to uncover the rich history, captivating landscapes, and vibrant communities that make Cape Cod a beloved destination for travelers from around the world. Whether you're seeking cultural immersion, natural beauty, or simply the joy of wandering, let's embark on an unforgettable adventure through the captivating wonders of Cape Cod.

Cape Cod National Seashore
One of Cape Cod's crown jewels is the Cape Cod National Seashore, a pristine and protected stretch of coastline that encompasses 40 miles of sandy beaches,

dunes, marshes, and woodlands. Established in 1961, the Cape Cod National Seashore is a testament to the region's commitment to preserving its natural beauty and rich cultural heritage. This remarkable area offers visitors a chance to immerse themselves in the awe-inspiring landscapes and diverse ecosystems that define Cape Cod.

Spanning from Chatham to Provincetown, the Cape Cod National Seashore is a paradise for nature lovers and outdoor enthusiasts. Here, you can stroll along sandy shores, hike through towering dunes, observe wildlife in its natural habitat, and explore historical sites that tell the story of the region's past.

The beaches within the national seashore are some of the most picturesque and pristine on Cape Cod. Coast Guard Beach, Nauset Light Beach, and Marconi Beach are just a few of the beloved sandy stretches that attract visitors with their breathtaking beauty and crashing waves. Spend a day relaxing on the soft sand, swimming in the refreshing Atlantic waters, or embarking on a leisurely beachcombing adventure.

For those seeking a deeper connection with nature, the Cape Cod National Seashore offers a network of scenic trails that wind through its diverse landscapes. Hike along the Atlantic White Cedar Swamp Trail in Wellfleet and discover the beauty of a unique ecosystem. Traverse the Fort Hill Trail in Eastham and enjoy panoramic views of Nauset Marsh and the surrounding countryside. The trails provide opportunities to spot wildlife, admire vibrant wildflowers, and witness the ever-changing coastal vistas.

The Cape Cod National Seashore is not only a haven for nature enthusiasts but also a gateway to Cape Cod's rich cultural heritage. Explore the historic sites within the seashore, such as the Highland Light in Truro, which has guided ships along the coastline since 1797. Visit the Salt Pond Visitor Center in Eastham, where you can learn about the seashore's natural and cultural history through exhibits, films, and ranger-led programs.

As you venture through the Cape Cod National Seashore, take a moment to appreciate its significance as a protected area that showcases the delicate balance between human activities and the preservation of natural resources. Whether you're capturing breathtaking sunsets, embarking on nature walks, or delving into the stories of the past, the Cape Cod National Seashore is a must-visit destination that embodies the essence of Cape Cod's beauty and heritage.

Note: When visiting the Cape Cod National Seashore, be sure to follow park regulations and practice Leave No Trace principles to help preserve the integrity of this remarkable natural treasure for future generations to enjoy.

Historic Sites and Landmarks

Cape Cod is steeped in history, with a rich tapestry of stories that unfold through its historic sites and landmarks. From the days of early European settlement to its role in American maritime history, Cape Cod offers a fascinating glimpse into the past. Exploring the region's historic sites and landmarks allows you to step back in time and connect with the people and events that shaped Cape Cod's identity.

Here are some notable places that showcase the region's historical significance:
- **Pilgrim Monument (Provincetown):** Standing tall in Provincetown, the Pilgrim Monument commemorates the arrival of the Mayflower Pilgrims in 1620. Climb to the top for panoramic views of Provincetown and the surrounding Cape Cod landscape. The monument also houses a museum where you can learn about the Mayflower journey and the early days of European settlement in the region.
- **Plimoth Plantation (Plymouth):** While not technically on Cape Cod, a visit to Plimoth Plantation is a must for history enthusiasts. This living history museum offers a glimpse into the lives of the Pilgrims and the Wampanoag people who inhabited the area. Engage with costumed interpreters, explore recreated 17th-century villages, and gain a deeper understanding of the early colonial period.
- **Sandwich Glass Museum (Sandwich):** Step into the world of glassmaking at the Sandwich Glass Museum, located in the town of Sandwich. Discover the history of the Sandwich Glass Company, which produced renowned glassware from 1825 to 1888. Admire the exquisite glass pieces on display and watch live demonstrations of glassblowing techniques.
- **Cape Cod Museum of Art (Dennis):** Delve into Cape Cod's artistic heritage by visiting the

Cape Cod Museum of Art. The museum showcases a diverse collection of artwork created by local and regional artists. Explore the galleries featuring paintings, sculptures, and photography that capture the essence of Cape Cod's natural beauty and vibrant arts scene.

- **Highland Light (Truro):** Visit the Highland Light, also known as Cape Cod Light, located in Truro. This historic lighthouse, dating back to 1797, has guided ships along the treacherous coastline for centuries. Take a guided tour to learn about the light's fascinating history and enjoy sweeping views of the Atlantic Ocean and Cape Cod Bay.
- **Chatham Lighthouse (Chatham):** Located on the southeastern tip of Cape Cod, the Chatham Lighthouse has served as a beacon for sailors since 1808. Explore the grounds, learn about the history of the lighthouse, and enjoy the picturesque views of Chatham Harbor and the Atlantic Ocean.
- **Crosby Mansion (Brewster):** Step into the grandeur of the Gilded Age by visiting Crosby Mansion, a historic mansion in Brewster. Take a guided tour of this magnificent estate, which showcases exquisite architectural details and offers a glimpse into the opulent lifestyle of the early 20th century.

These are just a few examples of the many historic sites and landmarks that await exploration on Cape Cod. Each one provides a window into the region's past, offering insights into its cultural heritage, maritime traditions, and architectural legacy. As you visit these sites, let their stories transport you back in time and deepen your appreciation for Cape Cod's rich history.

Lighthouses of Cape Cod

Cape Cod is renowned for its picturesque lighthouses, which have long served as beacons of safety along the rugged coastline. These iconic structures not only guide ships and mariners but also hold a special place in the region's maritime history and charm. Exploring the lighthouses of Cape Cod is a captivating journey that allows you to appreciate their architectural beauty, learn about their fascinating stories, and enjoy breathtaking views of the surrounding landscapes. Here are some notable lighthouses that you should include in your Cape Cod adventure:

- **Highland Light (Truro):** Perched atop the bluffs of Cape Cod's outermost point, Highland Light, also known as Cape Cod Light, is one of the most famous and picturesque lighthouses in New England. Dating back to 1857, it has played a crucial role in guiding ships through the treacherous waters off Cape Cod. Take a guided tour to learn about its rich history and enjoy panoramic views of the Atlantic Ocean and Cape Cod Bay.
- **Nauset Light (Eastham):** Recognizable for its distinctive red and white stripes, Nauset Light is a beloved symbol of Cape Cod. Originally located in Chatham, it was moved to Eastham in 1923. This charming lighthouse, featured on many postcards and photographs,

offers visitors a glimpse into the region's maritime past. Explore the grounds, learn about its significance, and capture stunning views of the Atlantic coastline.
- **Chatham Lighthouse (Chatham):** Standing at the entrance to Chatham Harbor, the Chatham Lighthouse has guided ships since 1808. The current tower, constructed in 1877, replaced the original lighthouse that was destroyed by erosion. Take a walk along Lighthouse Beach, marvel at the picturesque scene, and learn about the lighthouse's vital role in maritime navigation.
- **Race Point Light (Provincetown):** Located at the tip of Cape Cod in Provincetown, Race Point Light has been a guiding light for mariners since 1816. Surrounded by dunes and expansive beaches, this lighthouse offers a scenic backdrop for exploration. Visit the Cape Cod Highland Lighthouse Interpretive Center nearby to delve into the history and significance of the lighthouse.
- **Wings Neck Lighthouse (Pocasset):** While not technically on Cape Cod, Wings Neck Lighthouse in Pocasset is worth a visit for lighthouse enthusiasts. Situated on a scenic peninsula overlooking Buzzards Bay, this beautifully restored lighthouse showcases its rich history and offers stunning views of the water and surrounding landscapes.

As you visit these lighthouses, keep in mind that some may be open for tours, allowing you to climb to the top and experience the breathtaking vistas from the lantern room. Additionally, the surrounding areas often offer opportunities for beachcombing, nature walks, and picnics. Capture the beauty of these iconic structures through photographs or simply take a moment to soak in the peaceful atmosphere and appreciate their significance in Cape Cod's maritime heritage.

Note: Lighthouse accessibility and visitor facilities may vary, so it's advisable to check their operating hours and tour availability before your visit.

Museums and Art Galleries

Cape Cod is not only a haven for natural beauty and outdoor adventures but also a thriving hub of artistic expression and cultural heritage. The region is home to a diverse array of museums and art galleries that celebrate the arts, history, and local talent. Exploring these cultural institutions allows you to delve deeper into Cape Cod's creative spirit and gain a deeper appreciation for its vibrant arts scene. Here are some notable museums and art galleries to include in your Cape Cod itinerary:

- **Cape Cod Museum of Art (Dennis):** Situated in Dennis, the Cape Cod Museum of Art is a treasure trove for art enthusiasts. The museum showcases a wide range of artwork by local, regional, and nationally recognized artists, including paintings, sculptures, ceramics, and photography. Explore the galleries and immerse yourself in Cape Cod's artistic heritage.
- **Provincetown Art Association and Museum (Provincetown):** Provincetown has long been a haven for artists, and the Provincetown Art

Association and Museum (PAAM) embodies the town's creative energy. PAAM features rotating exhibitions that highlight the works of renowned local artists and hosts various events, workshops, and lectures. Take the time to browse through the galleries and discover the diverse artistic expressions that have shaped Provincetown's artistic legacy.
- **Heritage Museums & Gardens (Sandwich):** Located in Sandwich, Heritage Museums & Gardens offers a unique blend of art, nature, and history. Explore the expansive gardens, which feature a vast collection of plants and outdoor sculptures. Visit the Automobile Gallery, showcasing vintage cars, and the American Folk Art Gallery, which exhibits an impressive collection of folk art and artifacts.
- **Sandwich Glass Museum (Sandwich):** Discover the fascinating history of glassmaking at the Sandwich Glass Museum. Learn about the town's role in the glass industry and marvel at the exquisite glass pieces on display. Watch live demonstrations of glassblowing techniques and gain a deeper understanding of the artistry behind this delicate craft.
- **Cahoon Museum of American Art (Cotuit):** Nestled in Cotuit, the Cahoon Museum of American Art celebrates the rich heritage of American art. The museum features a diverse collection of artwork spanning various periods and styles, including paintings, sculptures, and works on paper. Indulge in the world of

American art and appreciate the talents of both established and emerging artists.
- **Falmouth Museums on the Green (Falmouth):** Step into Falmouth's history at the Falmouth Museums on the Green. The museums comprise two historic houses that showcase the town's past through exhibits, artifacts, and interactive displays. Learn about Falmouth's maritime heritage, explore its colonial history, and gain insights into the lives of its early residents.
- **Wellfleet Historical Society Museum (Wellfleet):** For a glimpse into Wellfleet's past, visit the Wellfleet Historical Society Museum. Located in a former schoolhouse, the museum houses exhibits that highlight the town's history, including its maritime traditions, whaling industry, and art colony. Explore the artifacts and photographs that provide a window into Wellfleet's cultural heritage.

These are just a few examples of the many museums and art galleries that await exploration on Cape Cod. Each institution offers a unique perspective on the region's artistic legacy, cultural heritage, and historical significance. Plan your visits accordingly, immerse yourself in the world of creativity and knowledge, and let Cape Cod's vibrant arts and culture scene inspire you.

Shopping and Dining

Cape Cod not only offers captivating natural beauty and rich history but also a delightful shopping and dining experience. Whether you're seeking unique souvenirs, local craftsmanship, or delectable culinary delights, the region's charming towns and villages provide a plethora of options to satisfy your shopping and dining desires. Here's a glimpse into the shopping and dining scene of Cape Cod:

Shopping:

Cape Cod is dotted with quaint shops, boutiques, and art galleries where you can find a wide range of treasures. From handcrafted jewelry and artisanal crafts to local artwork and Cape Cod-themed merchandise, there's something for every taste. Explore the vibrant main streets and village centers of towns like Chatham, Provincetown, and Hyannis, where you'll discover an eclectic mix of shops offering unique products. Don't forget to visit local farmers' markets and specialty food stores to sample the region's culinary delights, including fresh seafood, homemade jams, and Cape Cod cranberry products.

Antiquing:

If you're a fan of antiques and vintage finds, Cape Cod has numerous antique shops and markets to explore. You'll uncover a treasure trove of antique furniture, vintage clothing, collectibles, and one-of-a-kind items that reflect the region's history and charm. Towns like Sandwich, Dennis, and Brewster are known for their antique shops, where you can spend hours browsing through the carefully curated collections.

Dining:

Cape Cod's culinary scene is a delightful blend of fresh seafood, farm-to-table cuisine, and international flavors. From casual seafood shacks and charming cafes to upscale restaurants and waterfront eateries, there's a dining experience to suit every palate. Indulge in succulent lobster rolls, clam chowder, and freshly caught fish. Savor farm-fresh produce, locally sourced ingredients, and innovative dishes prepared by talented chefs. Many restaurants offer picturesque views of the ocean, harbor, or quaint village streets, enhancing your dining experience with stunning vistas.

Cape Cod Farmers' Markets:

Immerse yourself in the local food culture by visiting the Cape Cod farmers' markets. These markets offer a vibrant display of fresh produce, artisanal products, baked goods, and homemade treats. Interact with local farmers, bakers, and artisans as you explore the stalls, and sample the flavors of Cape Cod. The farmers' markets provide an opportunity to support local producers and experience the region's agricultural heritage.

Cape Cod Breweries and Wineries:

For beer and wine enthusiasts, Cape Cod boasts a growing number of breweries and wineries. Take a tour of a local brewery and learn about the craft beer-making process while tasting a variety of brews.

Visit a winery and indulge in wine tastings, savoring the unique flavors crafted from locally grown grapes.

Cape Cod Creameries and Sweet Treats:

Don't forget to satisfy your sweet tooth with a visit to Cape Cod's creameries and confectioneries. Indulge in homemade ice cream, where you'll find a myriad of flavors inspired by the region's bounty, including cranberry, salted caramel, and Cape Codder (a blend of cranberry and vodka). Treat yourself to delectable chocolates, fudge, and other handmade sweets that capture the essence of Cape Cod.

As you explore the shopping and dining scene of Cape Cod, take the time to interact with local shop owners, artisans, and chefs, who are passionate about their craft and eager to share their stories. Embrace the charm and hospitality of Cape Cod as you discover unique treasures, savor delicious meals, and create lasting memories.

Entertainment and Nightlife

While Cape Cod is renowned for its natural beauty and historical attractions, it also offers a vibrant entertainment and nightlife scene that caters to a variety of interests. From live music performances and theater productions to lively bars and waterfront venues, there are plenty of options to keep you entertained after the sun goes down. Here's a glimpse into the entertainment and nightlife offerings on Cape Cod:

Live Music Venues:

Cape Cod is home to numerous venues that showcase live music performances across a range of genres. From intimate coffeehouses and cozy pubs to larger concert halls and outdoor amphitheaters, there's something for every music lover. Enjoy local bands, talented musicians, and visiting artists as they take the stage, providing a memorable evening of entertainment. Check out the schedules of venues like The Beachcomber in Wellfleet, The Melody Tent in Hyannis, and Payomet Performing Arts Center in North Truro for an array of musical performances throughout the year.

Theater and Performing Arts:

If you're a fan of theater and performing arts, Cape Cod has a thriving arts scene that offers a variety of stage productions. The region is home to several professional theaters and community theater groups, presenting a diverse range of plays, musicals, and performances. From classic dramas and comedies to contemporary productions, you'll find a wealth of talent and creativity on display. Check out venues such as the Cape Playhouse in Dennis and the Provincetown Theater in Provincetown for an enriching theatrical experience.

Waterfront Dining and Bars:

Cape Cod's coastal setting provides the perfect backdrop for waterfront dining and lively bars. Many restaurants and bars offer stunning views of the ocean, bays, and harbors, allowing you to enjoy a delicious meal or refreshing drink while taking in the scenic beauty. Whether you're looking for a romantic dinner, a lively pub atmosphere, or a relaxed beachfront spot, you'll find a wide range of options to suit your preferences. Popular areas for waterfront dining and bars include Hyannis Harbor, Provincetown's Commercial Street, and Chatham's Main Street.

Nightclubs and Dance Halls:

For those seeking a more energetic and vibrant nightlife experience, Cape Cod has a selection of nightclubs and dance halls. These venues often feature live DJs, themed nights, and a lively atmosphere where you can dance the night away. Whether you're into electronic music, live bands, or a mix of genres, you'll find venues in towns like Falmouth, Mashpee, and Provincetown that cater to various tastes and preferences.

Comedy Clubs:

If you're in the mood for laughter, Cape Cod has a few comedy clubs that host stand-up performances and comedy shows. Sit back, relax, and enjoy the comedic talents of both local and nationally recognized comedians as they entertain you with their wit and humor. Check out comedy clubs in towns like Hyannis and Dennis for a night of laughter and entertainment.

Festivals and Events:

Cape Cod hosts a variety of festivals and events throughout the year, offering a unique blend of entertainment, culture, and community celebration. From art festivals and food fairs to music festivals and seasonal events, there's always something happening on Cape Cod. Check the event calendars and local listings to discover upcoming festivals and events that align with your interests.

Whether you prefer a laid-back evening by the waterfront, a night filled with live music, or an energetic dance floor, Cape Cod's entertainment and nightlife scene has something for everyone. Embrace the lively atmosphere, mingle with locals and visitors alike, and create unforgettable memories as you immerse yourself in the vibrant nightlife of Cape Cod.

CAPE COD TRAVEL GUIDE

Outdoor Adventures

Cape Cod is a paradise for outdoor enthusiasts, offering a wealth of opportunities to explore its natural wonders and engage in thrilling outdoor activities. From pristine beaches and picturesque trails to scenic waterways and wildlife-rich preserves, the region invites you to embark on unforgettable outdoor adventures. Whether you're seeking adrenaline-pumping experiences or serene moments in nature, Cape Cod has it all. Get ready to discover the great outdoors with a wide array of activities to suit every interest and skill level.

As you venture into Cape Cod's outdoor playground, prepare to be mesmerized by its breathtaking landscapes, diverse ecosystems, and abundant wildlife. From the rugged beauty of the Cape Cod National Seashore to the tranquil ponds and marshes that dot the landscape, the region offers a captivating tapestry of natural wonders to explore.

From hiking scenic trails and biking along coastal routes to kayaking through pristine waterways and embarking on thrilling fishing excursions, this section will guide you through the myriad of activities available. You'll also find tips on equipment, safety considerations, and must-visit locations to make the most of your outdoor experiences.

Whether you're a seasoned outdoor enthusiast or a beginner seeking new adventures, Cape Cod provides the perfect playground to satisfy your thirst for exploration. So, lace up your hiking boots, pack your swimsuit and sunscreen, and prepare to embark on an unforgettable journey through Cape Cod's outdoor wonders. Let the natural beauty of this coastal paradise ignite your sense of adventure and create lasting memories of outdoor exploration.

Hiking and Biking Trails

Cape Cod's scenic landscapes and diverse terrain make it an ideal destination for hiking and biking enthusiasts. With an extensive network of trails that wind through forests, dunes, marshes, and coastal areas, the region offers endless opportunities to immerse yourself in nature and experience the beauty of Cape Cod up close. Lace up your hiking boots or hop on your bike as we explore some of the most picturesque trails that await you on the Cape.

1. **Cape Cod Rail Trail:** Spanning 22 miles from Dennis to Wellfleet, the Cape Cod Rail Trail is a popular route for both hikers and bikers. Following the path of the old railroad, this scenic trail takes you through picturesque landscapes, charming towns, and serene natural areas. Enjoy the shade of canopied sections, cross charming bridges, and discover hidden gems along the way. The trail is

well-maintained and offers various access points, making it suitable for all skill levels.
2. **National Seashore Trails:** The Cape Cod National Seashore is a treasure trove of natural beauty and diverse ecosystems. The seashore boasts several hiking trails that showcase the region's stunning coastal landscapes and unique flora and fauna. Explore the Great Island Trail in Wellfleet, which offers a seven-mile loop through salt marshes, dunes, and secluded beaches. The Fort Hill Trail in Eastham provides panoramic views of Nauset Marsh and the Atlantic Ocean. These trails offer a chance to connect with the pristine natural beauty of Cape Cod's coastline.
3. **Nickerson State Park:** Located in Brewster, Nickerson State Park is a sprawling parkland with an extensive trail system. The park offers over 400 acres of forests, kettle ponds, and picturesque scenery. Hike or bike along the park's trails, such as the eight-mile Cape Cod Pathway, which meanders through pine forests and around crystal-clear ponds. Take a refreshing swim in one of the park's freshwater ponds or simply relax in the peaceful natural surroundings.
4. **Wellfleet Bay Wildlife Sanctuary:** For nature lovers and bird enthusiasts, the Wellfleet Bay Wildlife Sanctuary is a must-visit destination. Explore the sanctuary's trails, which wind through diverse habitats, including salt marshes, woodlands, and coastal dunes. Keep an eye out for various bird species, including

herons, egrets, and ospreys. The sanctuary also offers guided walks and educational programs for visitors of all ages.
5. **Shining Sea Bikeway:** Stretching from North Falmouth to Woods Hole, the Shining Sea Bikeway is a scenic 11.5-mile trail that hugs the coastline. Enjoy breathtaking ocean views, pedal past salt marshes and cranberry bogs, and discover charming seaside towns along the way. The trail provides an enjoyable and family-friendly biking experience, with several access points and amenities along the route.

Before embarking on any hiking or biking adventure, it's essential to be prepared and follow safety guidelines. Wear appropriate footwear, carry water and snacks, and be aware of any trail regulations or closures. Additionally, consider the season and weather conditions when planning your outdoor activities.

Cape Cod's hiking and biking trails offer a wonderful opportunity to reconnect with nature, enjoy scenic vistas, and appreciate the region's natural diversity. So, grab your hiking boots or hop on your bike, and get ready to explore the beauty that awaits you on the trails of Cape Cod.

Kayaking and Canoeing

With its vast coastline, serene ponds, and winding waterways, Cape Cod provides an idyllic setting for kayaking and canoeing adventures. Whether you're an experienced paddler or a novice looking to try something new, exploring Cape Cod's waterways by kayak or canoe offers a unique perspective and a chance to connect with the region's natural beauty. Get ready to grab a paddle and immerse yourself in the tranquility of Cape Cod's aquatic wonders.

1. **Saltwater Kayaking:** Cape Cod's coastline offers endless opportunities for saltwater kayaking. Explore the calm waters of bays and estuaries, paddle along pristine beaches, and discover hidden coves and islands. Launch your kayak from various access points, such as Wellfleet Harbor, Barnstable Harbor, or the calm waters of Pleasant Bay. Keep an eye out for coastal wildlife, including seals, shorebirds, and even the occasional sighting of dolphins or whales. Whether you choose a guided tour or venture out on your own, saltwater kayaking on Cape Cod promises a memorable and scenic experience.
2. **Freshwater Paddling:** Cape Cod is dotted with picturesque ponds and lakes that are perfect for freshwater kayaking and canoeing. Nickerson State Park in Brewster, Shawme-Crowell State Forest in Sandwich, and the numerous kettle ponds found throughout the region provide peaceful and serene settings for paddling. Glide across the clear waters, take in the surrounding natural beauty, and perhaps even dip your toes in for a refreshing swim. These tranquil freshwater spots offer a relaxing and rejuvenating experience for paddlers of all skill levels.
3. **Cape Cod Canal:** The Cape Cod Canal presents a unique opportunity for kayakers and canoeists to experience the power and beauty

of the tidal currents. The canal, which connects Cape Cod Bay and Buzzards Bay, offers a challenging yet rewarding paddling experience. Take on the currents as you paddle along the canal's scenic banks, enjoying views of passing boats, fishing opportunities, and the chance to spot marine life such as seals and seabirds. It's essential to be mindful of the canal's strong currents and plan your paddle according to tidal patterns for a safe and enjoyable experience.

4. **Guided Tours and Rentals:** If you're new to kayaking or prefer the expertise of a guide, Cape Cod has a range of guided tours and rental options available. Join a guided kayaking excursion led by experienced instructors who will provide insights into the local ecology, history, and wildlife. Rental shops throughout the region offer kayaks, canoes, and equipment for those who prefer to explore at their own pace.

Before heading out on the water, ensure you have the necessary safety equipment, including personal flotation devices (PFDs), and familiarize yourself with local regulations and guidelines. It's also important to be mindful of the environment and practice Leave No Trace principles, respecting the delicate ecosystems and wildlife habitats that make Cape Cod so special.

Kayaking and canoeing on Cape Cod offer a unique way to discover the region's natural wonders, from its pristine beaches and peaceful ponds to its captivating coastal estuaries. So, grab your paddle, embrace the serenity of the water, and embark on a memorable aquatic adventure on Cape Cod.

Fishing and Boating

Cape Cod's abundant waters provide a haven for fishing and boating enthusiasts. Whether you're an avid angler seeking the thrill of the catch or simply looking to enjoy a leisurely day on the water, Cape Cod offers a wide range of fishing and boating opportunities. From deep-sea fishing adventures to peaceful excursions on tranquil ponds and rivers, get ready to cast your line and set sail as we explore the fishing and boating experiences that await you on the Cape.

1. **Deep-Sea Fishing:** Cape Cod is renowned for its excellent deep-sea fishing opportunities. Charter a fishing boat and venture out into the Atlantic Ocean in pursuit of trophy fish like striped bass, bluefish, tuna, or even the prized Atlantic cod. Experienced captains and crews will guide you to the best fishing grounds, provide equipment and bait, and offer valuable tips and techniques to enhance your chances of a successful catch. Whether you're a seasoned angler or a novice looking to try deep-sea fishing for the first time, Cape Cod's deep waters offer an exhilarating fishing experience.

2. **Inshore and Fly Fishing:** If you prefer a more intimate fishing experience, Cape Cod's inshore waters and estuaries provide ample opportunities for inshore and fly fishing. Wade into the shallows, cast your line from a kayak, or fish from the shore as you target species

like striped bass, bluefish, flounder, and more. The region's marshes, tidal flats, and secluded coves offer an abundance of fishing spots to explore. Consider hiring a local fishing guide who can provide expert knowledge of the area and help you navigate the best fishing grounds.

3. **Boating and Sailing:** Cape Cod's picturesque coastline and numerous harbors and marinas make it an ideal destination for boating and sailing enthusiasts. Rent a powerboat, sailboat, or catamaran and cruise along the coast, enjoying panoramic views and the freedom to explore at your own pace. Visit the charming harbors of Provincetown, Chatham, or Hyannis, and anchor in secluded coves for a peaceful day on the water. Whether you're a seasoned sailor or a novice boater, Cape Cod's calm bays, protected harbors, and open waters offer an array of boating experiences to suit every skill level.

4. **Kayak and Canoe Fishing:** Combine the tranquility of paddling with the excitement of fishing by trying kayak or canoe fishing. Cape Cod's scenic ponds, lakes, and calm rivers provide excellent opportunities for kayak and canoe fishing. Paddle to secluded fishing spots, navigate narrow waterways, and enjoy the peaceful surroundings as you cast your line for bass, trout, pickerel, and more. Ensure you have the appropriate fishing gear and equipment designed for kayak or canoe fishing, as well as a valid fishing license.

Golfing and Tennis

For those who enjoy sports and outdoor recreation, Cape Cod offers excellent opportunities for golfing and tennis enthusiasts. With its picturesque landscapes and a variety of world-class courses and tennis facilities, the region is a haven for both leisure players and competitive athletes. Whether you're looking to tee off on lush fairways or sharpen your skills on the tennis court, Cape Cod provides a delightful setting for sports enthusiasts to enjoy their favorite pastimes.

1. **Golfing:** Cape Cod boasts numerous golf courses that cater to players of all skill levels. From championship courses designed by renowned architects to scenic seaside links, golfers can find a range of options to suit their preferences. Enjoy breathtaking views of the ocean, tranquil ponds, and rolling hills as you navigate the fairways and greens. Some notable golf courses on Cape Cod include the Ocean Course at The Club at New Seabury in Mashpee, Highland Links in Truro, and Cape Cod National Golf Club in Brewster. Whether you're a seasoned golfer or a beginner looking to learn the game, Cape Cod's golf courses offer a memorable experience in a stunning natural setting.
2. **Tennis:** Cape Cod features several tennis clubs and facilities that provide opportunities for players of all ages and skill levels. Whether you prefer singles, doubles, or even mixed doubles, you'll find well-maintained courts and welcoming communities to enjoy a game of tennis. Many clubs offer lessons,

clinics, and tournaments, providing opportunities for players to improve their skills and engage in friendly competition. Consider visiting the Mid-Cape Racquet & Health Club in South Yarmouth or the Dennis Highlands Tennis Complex in Dennis for exceptional tennis experiences on Cape Cod. In addition to traditional golf and tennis, Cape Cod also offers a range of alternative sports and recreational activities to keep you active and entertained. These include:

- **Disc Golf:** Try your hand at disc golf, a fun and challenging sport that combines elements of frisbee and golf. Several disc golf courses are scattered throughout Cape Cod, offering a unique and enjoyable outdoor experience for players of all ages.
- **Miniature Golf:** Cape Cod is known for its family-friendly miniature golf courses. Putt your way through creatively designed courses featuring waterfalls, windmills, and other whimsical obstacles. It's a perfect activity for a fun-filled day with family and friends.
- **Pickleball:** Join the growing popularity of pickleball, a paddle sport that combines elements of tennis, badminton, and ping pong. Many recreational facilities on Cape Cod now offer pickleball courts, allowing enthusiasts to engage in this fast-paced and exciting sport.

Whether you're a golf enthusiast seeking challenging fairways, a tennis aficionado looking for a friendly match, or someone seeking alternative recreational activities, Cape Cod has something to offer. With its scenic landscapes, welcoming communities, and a range of sporting facilities, the region invites you to engage in outdoor sports and experience the joy of playing against the backdrop of Cape Cod's natural beauty.

Whale Watching

Cape Cod is renowned as one of the premier whale-watching destinations in the United States, offering an extraordinary opportunity to witness these majestic creatures up close in their natural habitat. Every year, numerous species of whales, including humpback whales, finback whales, and minke whales, migrate to the waters off Cape Cod to feed and play. If you're a nature enthusiast or simply captivated by the beauty of marine life, a whale-watching excursion is a must-do experience during your visit to Cape Cod.

1. **Whale Species:** Cape Cod's waters are home to an impressive diversity of whale species. Humpback whales are among the most commonly spotted, known for their spectacular breaches and graceful movements. These gentle giants can reach lengths of up to 50 feet and are famous for their haunting songs. Finback whales, the second-largest whale species on the planet, are also frequently sighted off the coast of Cape Cod. With their sleek bodies and distinctive features, they are a sight to behold. Minke whales, known for their smaller size and playful nature, are often encountered during whale-watching excursions as well.
2. **Whale-Watching Tours:** Numerous whale-watching tour operators in Cape Cod

offer guided excursions led by experienced naturalists who provide insights into whale behavior, marine ecosystems, and conservation efforts. These tours typically depart from various locations, such as Provincetown, Barnstable, or Hyannis, and take you out to the whale feeding grounds aboard specially designed boats equipped with observation decks. The duration of the tours can range from a few hours to a full day, allowing ample time for sightings and educational experiences.
3. **Best Time for Whale Watching:** The prime time for whale watching on Cape Cod is generally from April to October when the whales migrate to the area in search of abundant food sources. During this period, you have the highest chance of encountering these magnificent creatures. However, peak whale activity often occurs in the summer months of June, July, and August. It's advisable to check with local tour operators or visitor centers for the most up-to-date information on whale sightings and tour availability.
4. **Code of Conduct:** While whale watching is an incredible experience, it's important to practice responsible and respectful behavior to ensure the well-being of the whales and their natural habitat. Follow guidelines provided by the tour operators, such as maintaining a safe distance from the whales, avoiding sudden or loud noises, and refraining from throwing anything into the water. By adhering to these

guidelines, you can help protect the whales and contribute to their conservation.

Whale watching on Cape Cod offers a captivating and unforgettable experience, allowing you to witness the magnificence of these gentle giants in their natural environment. From the excitement of spotting a spout on the horizon to witnessing the grace of a breaching whale, each moment is filled with awe and wonder. So, embark on a whale-watching adventure and create memories that will last a lifetime as you connect with the captivating marine world off Cape Cod's shores.

Camping and RV Parks

For those who seek a closer connection to nature, Cape Cod offers a range of camping and RV park options that allow you to immerse yourself in the region's natural beauty. Whether you prefer pitching a tent under the stars or enjoying the comforts of your own recreational vehicle, camping on Cape Cod provides a unique and memorable outdoor experience.

1. **Campgrounds:** Cape Cod features several campgrounds that cater to different camping preferences. From rustic and primitive sites to more developed campgrounds with modern amenities, there's something for everyone. Many campgrounds offer facilities such as restrooms, showers, picnic areas, and campfire pits. Some even provide recreational activities like hiking trails, swimming areas, and organized events. Consider popular campgrounds like Nickerson State Park in Brewster, Shawme-Crowell State Forest in Sandwich, or Scusset Beach State Reservation

in Sagamore for a memorable camping experience.
2. **RV Parks:** If you prefer the convenience and comforts of RV camping, Cape Cod offers a variety of RV parks and resorts. These parks typically provide spacious sites with amenities like full hookups, dump stations, Wi-Fi access, and on-site laundry facilities. Some RV parks also feature additional amenities such as swimming pools, playgrounds, and recreational facilities. Bay View Campground in Bourne, Cape Cod Campresort and Cabins in Falmouth, and Atlantic Oaks Campground in Eastham are among the popular options for RV enthusiasts visiting Cape Cod.
3. **Camping in National and State Parks:** Cape Cod is home to several national and state parks that offer camping opportunities amidst beautiful natural surroundings. The Cape Cod National Seashore, managed by the National Park Service, provides campgrounds like the Salt Pond Visitor Center Campground and the North of Highland Camping Area. These campgrounds offer a unique coastal camping experience within the protected seashore. Additionally, state parks such as Shawme-Crowell State Forest and Nickerson State Park mentioned earlier also provide camping facilities within their boundaries.
4. **Reservations and Permits:** It's important to plan ahead and make reservations for camping or RV sites, especially during the peak summer season. Popular campgrounds and RV

parks tend to fill up quickly, so securing your spot in advance is recommended. Some campgrounds operate on a first-come, first-served basis, while others require reservations. Be sure to check the specific reservation policies and availability of the campground or RV park you plan to visit. Additionally, certain areas may require permits or passes for camping, so it's essential to check the requirements beforehand.

Camping and RV parks on Cape Cod provide the opportunity to disconnect from the hustle and bustle of daily life and immerse yourself in the region's natural splendor. Whether you're roasting marshmallows around a campfire, enjoying the peacefulness of the outdoors, or waking up to the sounds of birds chirping, camping on Cape Cod offers a rejuvenating and memorable experience for outdoor enthusiasts. So, pack your camping gear or hop in your RV and embark on an adventure that combines comfort and serenity amidst Cape Cod's breathtaking landscapes.

CAPE COD TRAVEL GUIDE

Day Trips and Excursions

While Cape Cod itself is a treasure trove of attractions and natural wonders, it also serves as a gateway to an array of captivating destinations within reach. Embarking on day trips and excursions from Cape Cod allows you to expand your horizons and explore the surrounding areas, unveiling new adventures and discoveries. Whether you're seeking historical landmarks, scenic beauty, or cultural experiences, these day trips promise to enhance your Cape Cod travel itinerary and provide a broader perspective of the region.

Martha's Vineyard

Distance from Cape Cod: Approximately 7 miles (11.3 km) southeast of Falmouth, Massachusetts

GPS Coordinates:

- Woods Hole Ferry Terminal (Falmouth): 41.5246° N, 70.6723° W
- Vineyard Haven Ferry Terminal (Martha's Vineyard): 41.4539° N, 70.6033° W

Martha's Vineyard is a captivating island located just a short ferry ride away from Cape Cod. Known for its pristine beaches, charming towns, and picturesque landscapes, Martha's Vineyard offers a unique blend of natural beauty, cultural richness, and relaxed island vibes. Embarking on a day trip to Martha's Vineyard allows you to explore the island's distinct character and fully experience its inviting atmosphere firsthand.

To begin your journey, head to the Woods Hole Ferry Terminal in Falmouth, Massachusetts. From here, you can catch a ferry that will transport you across the sparkling waters of Vineyard Sound to the Vineyard Haven Ferry Terminal on Martha's Vineyard. The ferry ride itself is a scenic experience, providing panoramic views of the coastline and the surrounding ocean.

Once you arrive on Martha's Vineyard, a world of exploration awaits. Here are some highlights to consider during your day trip:

1. **Beaches:** Martha's Vineyard boasts several stunning beaches where you can relax, soak up the sun, and enjoy the refreshing ocean breeze. From the popular and family-friendly State Beach in Oak Bluffs to the serene and picturesque South Beach in Edgartown, the

island offers a range of coastal gems to suit your preferences.

2. **Towns and Villages:** Each town on Martha's Vineyard has its own distinctive character and charm. Explore the colorful gingerbread cottages and lively waterfront of Oak Bluffs, wander through the quaint streets of Edgartown with its historic architecture, or visit the laid-back and artistic community of Vineyard Haven. Stroll along the main streets, browse boutique shops, sample local cuisine, and soak up the vibrant island atmosphere.

3. **Aquinnah Cliffs:** Located on the western tip of Martha's Vineyard, the Aquinnah Cliffs, also known as the Gay Head Cliffs, offer breathtaking views and unique geological formations. The vibrant clay cliffs stand tall against the backdrop of the Atlantic Ocean, creating a mesmerizing landscape. Take a scenic walk along the cliffs, visit the historic Gay Head Lighthouse, and learn about the indigenous Wampanoag culture at the nearby Aquinnah Cultural Center.

4. **Outdoor Activities:** Martha's Vineyard is a paradise for outdoor enthusiasts. Rent a bike and explore the island's network of scenic bike paths, go kayaking or paddleboarding in the calm waters of the island's ponds, or embark on a nature hike through the serene landscapes of the Manuel F. Correllus State Forest. The island offers numerous opportunities to connect with nature and enjoy outdoor adventures.

To return to Cape Cod, simply catch the ferry back from the Vineyard Haven Ferry Terminal to the Woods Hole Ferry Terminal in Falmouth. Keep in mind the ferry schedules to ensure a timely departure and arrival.

Visiting Martha's Vineyard on a day trip from Cape Cod allows you to experience the island's beauty, culture, and relaxed ambiance. From its pristine beaches to its charming towns and breathtaking landscapes, Martha's Vineyard promises an unforgettable excursion that will add an extra layer of exploration to your Cape Cod travel experience.

Nantucket Island

Distance from Cape Cod: Approximately 30 miles (48 km) south of Cape Cod
GPS Coordinates:

- Hyannis Harbor (Cape Cod): 41.6539° N, 70.2887° W
- Nantucket Steamship Authority Terminal (Nantucket): 41.2829° N, 70.0997° W

Nantucket Island, located just a short ferry ride away from Cape Cod, is a captivating destination known for its timeless beauty, rich maritime history, and idyllic charm. With its cobblestone streets, historic architecture, and pristine beaches, Nantucket offers a quintessential New England experience that is sure to enchant visitors. Embarking on a day trip to Nantucket allows you to fully experience the island's unique atmosphere and explore its many attractions.

To begin your journey, make your way to the Hyannis Harbor on Cape Cod. From here, you can catch a ferry that will transport you across the waters of Nantucket Sound to the Nantucket Steamship Authority Terminal. The ferry ride itself offers panoramic views of the ocean, providing a refreshing and scenic start to your Nantucket adventure.

Once you arrive on Nantucket Island, you'll be greeted by a charming and picturesque setting. Here are some highlights to consider during your day trip:

1. **Historic Downtown:** Nantucket's historic downtown area is a treasure trove of preserved architecture, quaint streets, and cultural landmarks. Take a leisurely stroll along cobblestone streets lined with 18th-century houses, visit the Whaling Museum to learn about the island's whaling history, and explore the Nantucket Atheneum, a beautiful public library. Don't forget to browse the local boutiques, art galleries, and restaurants that add to the town's vibrant atmosphere.

2. **Beaches:** Nantucket boasts some of the most beautiful beaches in the region, with pristine sand and clear waters. From the popular Jetties Beach, which offers amenities like lifeguards and a beachside restaurant, to the secluded and tranquil Dionis Beach, there's a beach to suit every preference. Spend some time relaxing on the sandy shores, swimming in the refreshing waters, or simply enjoying the coastal scenery.

3. **Sankaty Head Lighthouse:** Located on the eastern edge of the island, Sankaty Head

Lighthouse stands as an iconic symbol of Nantucket. This historic lighthouse offers breathtaking views of the coastline and the Atlantic Ocean. Take a walk along the bluff and admire the panoramic vistas, or explore the surrounding Sconset village, known for its charming rose-covered cottages.

4. **Nantucket Bike Paths:** Nantucket Island features an extensive network of bike paths that allow you to explore the island's natural beauty at your own pace. Rent a bike and pedal along the scenic paths, which traverse moors, forests, and coastal landscapes. The paths provide an opportunity to appreciate Nantucket's unique ecosystem and enjoy the tranquility of the island's natural surroundings.

To return to Cape Cod, catch the ferry back from the Nantucket Steamship Authority Terminal to the Hyannis Harbor. Be sure to check the ferry schedules to plan your departure and arrival accordingly.

A day trip to Nantucket Island from Cape Cod offers a glimpse into a world of timeless beauty, rich history, and coastal charm. From the cobblestone streets of the historic downtown area to the pristine beaches and picturesque lighthouses, Nantucket promises a memorable experience that captures the essence of New England's coastal allure. So, set sail for Nantucket and discover the magic of this enchanting island just a short distance from Cape Cod.

Provincetown

Distance from Cape Cod: Located at the tip of Cape Cod

GPS Coordinates: 42.0511° N, 70.1875° W

Provincetown, or P-town as it's commonly known, is a vibrant and eclectic town nestled at the very tip of Cape Cod. Renowned for its artistic community, LGBTQ+ inclusivity, and picturesque coastal setting, Provincetown offers a unique and lively atmosphere that attracts visitors from all walks of life. A day trip to Provincetown allows you to immerse yourself in its vibrant culture, explore its historic streets, and enjoy the natural beauty of its surroundings.

As you make your way to Provincetown, you'll encounter breathtaking views of the Cape Cod National Seashore, pristine beaches, and the iconic Cape Cod dunes. Here are some highlights to consider during your day trip:

1. **Commercial Street:** The heart and soul of Provincetown, Commercial Street, is a lively thoroughfare lined with art galleries, boutique shops, restaurants, and entertainment venues. Take a leisurely stroll along this bustling street, soak in the vibrant atmosphere, and discover unique artwork, crafts, and souvenirs. Commercial Street also serves as the starting point for many events and parades, making it an exciting place to experience the town's festive spirit.

2. **Pilgrim Monument and Provincetown Museum:** Standing tall on High Pole Hill, the Pilgrim Monument is an iconic symbol of Provincetown. Climb the monument's 252-foot (77-meter) tower for panoramic views of the town and the surrounding coastline. Adjacent to the monument, you'll find the Provincetown Museum, which offers a fascinating insight

into the town's rich maritime history, its significance as the landing place of the Mayflower Pilgrims, and its vibrant art community.
3. **Provincetown Harbor:** Provincetown Harbor is a picturesque natural harbor that has played a significant role in the town's history. Take a scenic stroll along the waterfront, watch fishing boats return with their daily catch, or embark on a whale-watching excursion to witness the majestic creatures that frequent the area. The harbor offers a beautiful backdrop for leisurely walks, boat tours, and captivating sunsets.
4. **Art and Cultural Scene:** Provincetown has long been a haven for artists, writers, and creative individuals. Explore the town's numerous art galleries and studios, showcasing a diverse range of artistic styles and mediums. Visit the Provincetown Art Association and Museum to admire works by renowned artists or catch a performance at one of the town's theaters. Provincetown's rich artistic heritage is evident in its vibrant cultural offerings.

To reach Provincetown, you can drive along scenic Route 6, known as the "Mid-Cape Highway," which will take you directly to the town. Alternatively, you can also take a ferry from various locations on Cape Cod, such as the town of Hyannis, for a scenic and leisurely journey across Cape Cod Bay.

A day trip to Provincetown offers a dynamic blend of artistic expression, rich history, and coastal charm. Whether you're strolling along Commercial Street, exploring the town's cultural offerings, or simply enjoying the beauty of its beaches and harbor, Provincetown promises an unforgettable experience that captures the essence of Cape Cod's unique spirit.

Plymouth

Distance from Cape Cod: Approximately 40 miles (64 km) northwest of Cape Cod

GPS Coordinates: 41.9584° N, 70.6673° W

Plymouth, Massachusetts, holds a special place in American history as the site of the first permanent English settlement in New England. Steeped in colonial heritage and renowned for its connection to the Pilgrims and the Mayflower voyage, Plymouth offers a captivating blend of history, culture, and natural beauty. A day trip to Plymouth allows you to step back in time and explore the roots of American history while enjoying the town's coastal charm.

As you venture into Plymouth, you'll discover a variety of attractions that highlight its historical significance and cultural treasures. Here are some highlights to consider during your day trip:

1. **Plymouth Rock:** A visit to Plymouth is incomplete without seeing Plymouth Rock, a symbol of the Mayflower Pilgrims' arrival in 1620. Located along the waterfront, this iconic rock is inscribed with the date "1620" and has become a significant historical landmark. While the rock itself may seem modest, its historical significance and the surrounding park make it a must-see attraction for history enthusiasts.

2. **Plimoth Patuxet Museums:** Embark on a journey to fully explore the captivating history

of the Pilgrims and the Wampanoag. Native American tribe at the Plimoth Patuxet Museums. The museum complex includes the Plimoth Plantation, a living history museum where you can interact with costumed interpreters and explore a recreated 17th-century English village and a Wampanoag homesite. Gain insight into the daily life, traditions, and challenges faced by the Pilgrims and the Native Americans.
3. **Mayflower II:** Step aboard the Mayflower II, a full-scale replica of the original Mayflower ship that carried the Pilgrims to Plymouth. Explore the decks, learn about the journey and hardships endured by the Pilgrims, and gain a deeper understanding of their historical significance. The Mayflower II offers a fascinating glimpse into the conditions faced by the early settlers.
4. **Plymouth Waterfront:** Take a leisurely stroll along the picturesque Plymouth Waterfront, lined with shops, restaurants, and stunning views of the harbor. Enjoy fresh seafood, browse local boutiques, and savor the coastal ambiance. The waterfront area also offers opportunities for scenic boat tours, fishing excursions, and beautiful views of the harbor and its surrounding landscapes.
5. **Plimoth Grist Mill:** Experience the authentic sights and sounds of a working 17th-century grist mill at the Plimoth Grist Mill. Learn about the process of grinding corn and witness the power of water as it turns the mill's

massive wheel. This historical attraction offers insight into the early agricultural practices of the Pilgrims and their reliance on mills for food production.

To reach Plymouth from Cape Cod, you can drive north on Route 3, which provides direct access to the town. Additionally, guided tours and transportation options are available for a convenient and informative day trip experience.

A day trip to Plymouth offers a fascinating journey back in time to the beginnings of American history. From standing on Plymouth Rock to exploring the living history museum and encountering the Mayflower replica, you'll gain a deeper appreciation for the Pilgrims' courage and the challenges they faced. Discover the town's historical treasures, enjoy its scenic waterfront, and savor the coastal charm of Plymouth—a place where history comes to life.

New Bedford

Distance from Cape Cod: Approximately 30 miles (48 km) east of Cape Cod

GPS Coordinates: 41.6362° N, 70.9342° W

Nestled along the southeastern coast of Massachusetts, New Bedford is a historic city with a rich maritime heritage. Known for its deep connection to the whaling industry and its cultural diversity, a day trip to New Bedford offers a unique blend of history, art, and coastal charm. Explore its fascinating museums, stroll along its picturesque waterfront, and delve into the stories that shaped this captivating city. Here are some highlights to consider during your day trip to New Bedford:

1. **New Bedford Whaling Museum:** Begin your journey at the renowned New Bedford Whaling Museum, which provides an immersive experience into the city's whaling history. Discover impressive exhibits showcasing whaling artifacts, including a life-size whale skeleton, scrimshaw artwork, and interactive displays. Gain insight into the industry's impact on New Bedford and its pivotal role in American maritime history.
2. **Historic District and Seaport Cultural District:** Take a leisurely walk through New Bedford's Historic District, filled with beautifully preserved 19th-century buildings. Admire the architectural gems, including stately homes, museums, and churches. Don't miss the Seaport Cultural District, where you can explore art galleries, boutique shops, and enjoy live performances. The district's cobblestone streets and charming atmosphere create a delightful ambiance for exploration.
3. **New Bedford Whaling National Historical Park:** Step into the past at the New Bedford Whaling National Historical Park, encompassing several blocks of historic streets and buildings. Take a self-guided walking tour to learn about the city's whaling era and the impact it had on its development. Visit the Seamen's Bethel, made famous by Herman Melville's novel "Moby-Dick," and the nearby Mariners' Home, which offers a glimpse into the lives of seafarers.

4. **Buttonwood Park Zoo:** For a family-friendly experience, visit the Buttonwood Park Zoo, home to a diverse collection of animals from around the world. Stroll through the beautifully landscaped grounds, observe fascinating creatures, and enjoy educational exhibits and interactive experiences. The zoo provides a delightful respite amidst New Bedford's urban setting.
5. **Fort Taber Park:** Explore the historic Fort Taber Park, located on Clark's Point. This coastal park offers panoramic views of Buzzards Bay and the entrance to New Bedford Harbor. Walk along the fort's ramparts, visit the museum inside the fort, and enjoy picnicking or relaxing in the park's scenic surroundings. Fort Taber Park is an ideal spot to soak up the coastal beauty and appreciate New Bedford's strategic maritime position.

To reach New Bedford from Cape Cod, you can drive westward on Route 6 and then head south on Route 140, which leads directly into the city. Public transportation options, such as buses, are also available for a convenient day trip experience.

A day trip to New Bedford unveils a captivating blend of maritime history, cultural diversity, and natural beauty. From exploring the whaling industry's legacy at the museum to strolling through the historic district and immersing yourself in the city's vibrant arts scene, New Bedford offers a multifaceted experience that celebrates its rich heritage. Embark on a journey of discovery, and let the stories of this remarkable city unfold before your eyes.

Hyannis and the Kennedy Legacy

Distance from Cape Cod: Located on Cape Cod itself

GPS Coordinates: 41.6519° N, 70.2867° W

Hyannis, a charming village located on Cape Cod, Massachusetts, holds a special place in American history as the beloved summer retreat of the Kennedy family. With its picturesque harbor, sandy beaches, and significant ties to the Kennedy legacy, a day trip to Hyannis offers a unique blend of coastal beauty and political history. Visit iconic landmarks, and learn about the influential Kennedy family's impact on both Hyannis and the nation.

Here are some highlights to consider during your day trip to Hyannis and the Kennedy Legacy:

1. **John F. Kennedy Hyannis Museum:** Begin your journey by visiting the John F. Kennedy Hyannis Museum, dedicated to preserving the memory of President John F. Kennedy and his connection to Cape Cod. Explore exhibits showcasing photographs, videos, and personal artifacts that chronicle the Kennedy family's time spent in Hyannis. Gain insight into their political achievements, personal lives, and the enduring legacy they left behind.

2. **Hyannis Harbor:** Stroll along the picturesque Hyannis Harbor, where you can enjoy the sight of boats bobbing in the water and soak in the coastal ambiance. Take a scenic harbor cruise or hop on a ferry to explore the nearby islands of Martha's Vineyard or Nantucket.

The harbor area also offers waterfront dining options, boutique shops, and the opportunity to relax on pristine beaches.

3. **Kennedy Compound:** While the Kennedy Compound itself is not open to the public, you can still catch a glimpse of this iconic location from a distance. Located in the nearby village of Hyannis Port, the compound served as the Kennedy family's summer residence and a gathering place for political discussions and family celebrations. Enjoy a scenic drive through the Hyannis Port neighborhood and appreciate the historical significance of this prominent landmark.
4. **St. Francis Xavier Church:** Visit St. Francis Xavier Church, the place of worship for the Kennedy family during their time in Hyannis. This beautiful church holds historical significance and provides a serene atmosphere for reflection and contemplation. Take a moment to appreciate the church's architectural beauty and the role it played in the Kennedy family's spiritual life.
5. **Main Street Hyannis:** Explore Main Street Hyannis, a vibrant downtown area filled with boutique shops, art galleries, restaurants, and cafes. Stroll along the charming streets, browse unique shops, and indulge in local cuisine. Main Street also features the Hyannis Village Green, where you can relax in the park, attend events, or catch a live performance during the summer months.

To reach Hyannis, you can drive along Route 6, the main highway that runs through Cape Cod. The village is easily accessible and offers ample parking facilities. Additionally, public transportation options, including buses and trains, connect Hyannis to other parts of Cape Cod and neighboring cities.

A day trip to Hyannis provides a unique opportunity to fully experience the beauty of Cape Cod while exploring the influential Kennedy legacy. From delving into the exhibits at the Hyannis Museum to experiencing the coastal charm of the harbor, Hyannis offers a captivating blend of history, natural beauty, and cultural attractions. Discover the connection between the Kennedy family and this beloved Cape Cod destination, and appreciate the enduring impact they left on both Hyannis and the nation.

Events and Festivals

Cape Cod is not only known for its scenic beauty and rich history but also for its vibrant and lively events and festivals. Throughout the year, the Cape comes alive with a variety of celebrations that showcase the region's cultural heritage, artistic talents, and community spirit. From traditional festivals steeped in history to lively music concerts and art exhibitions, there is always something exciting happening on Cape Cod.

Join in the festivities, and create lasting memories as you experience the dynamic events and festivals that make Cape Cod a vibrant destination for visitors and locals alike. Discover the diverse range of celebrations, mark your calendars, and get ready to join the festivities as we dive into the exciting world of Cape Cod's events and festivals.

Cape Cod Baseball League

Every summer, Cape Cod becomes a hotbed of baseball fever as the Cape Cod Baseball League takes center stage. Known as the premier amateur summer baseball league in the country, the Cape Cod Baseball League has a rich history dating back to 1885. This beloved league attracts top collegiate players from around the nation, providing them with a platform to showcase their skills in a competitive and prestigious environment.

The Cape Cod Baseball League offers an unparalleled opportunity to witness the stars of tomorrow in action today. With teams scattered across the Cape, from Bourne to Orleans, the league provides baseball enthusiasts with ample opportunities to catch a game and experience the excitement firsthand. From the crack of the bat to the roar of the crowd, the atmosphere at these games is electric, creating an unforgettable experience for spectators of all ages.

As you immerse yourself in the Cape Cod Baseball League, you'll witness the passion and dedication of these young athletes as they chase their dreams. From fastballs to curveballs, and home runs to diving catches, each game showcases the raw talent and determination of these up-and-coming baseball stars. Whether you're a die-hard baseball fan or simply appreciate the thrill of live sports, attending a Cape Cod Baseball League game is a must-do experience. Keep an eye on the league's schedule to plan your visit and catch a game at one of the iconic ballparks on Cape Cod. From the scenic backdrop of the Chatham Anglers to the historic field in Hyannis, each ballpark has its own unique charm and adds to the allure of the Cape Cod Baseball League experience. Remember to bring your baseball glove and wholeheartedly embrace the timeless traditions of the game. Treat yourself to the classic experience of savoring a hot dog and soda in the stands, while cheering on your favorite players.

The Cape Cod Baseball League not only provides entertainment but also contributes to the Cape's sense of community and pride. Locals and visitors come together to support their respective teams, creating a spirited atmosphere that adds to the magic of the games. Whether you're a longtime fan or a first-time spectator, the Cape Cod Baseball League offers an unparalleled opportunity to witness top-tier baseball talent, soak up the summer vibes, and become part of the Cape's baseball legacy.

So, grab your cap, don your team colors, and get ready to experience the thrill of America's pastime on Cape Cod. Join the passionate fans, soak in the sunshine, and root for the next generation of baseball stars as they take to the field in the Cape Cod Baseball League.

Summer Concerts and Performances

When the warm summer breeze sweeps across Cape Cod, it brings with it a symphony of captivating melodies and enchanting performances. From outdoor stages to intimate venues, Cape Cod comes alive with a vibrant lineup of summer concerts and performances that cater to a wide range of musical tastes and artistic expressions. Whether you're a fan of rock, jazz, classical, or folk, there is a concert or performance that will resonate with your soul.

Throughout the summer months, Cape Cod hosts an array of musical events that showcase local talent as well as renowned artists from around the world. From lively beach concerts to intimate acoustic sessions, the Cape's music scene offers something for everyone.

Picture yourself sitting under the stars, toes in the sand, as the sounds of live music fill the air, creating an atmosphere of pure joy and relaxation.

In addition to concerts, the performing arts take center stage with theatrical productions, dance performances, and comedy shows that captivate audiences of all ages. From renowned theater companies to local community troupes, Cape Cod offers a diverse and vibrant performing arts scene. Step into the enchanting world of theater, witness breathtaking dance routines, and find yourself laughing uncontrollably at a comedy show.

One of the highlights of Cape Cod's summer concert and performance scene is the Cape Cod Melody Tent. This iconic venue, located in Hyannis, hosts a lineup of nationally acclaimed artists throughout the summer season. The unique circular tent design creates an intimate and immersive experience, allowing the audience to feel connected to the performers on stage. Beyond the Melody Tent, various parks, beaches, and outdoor venues become stages for free concerts and performances. Pack a picnic, bring a blanket or a beach chair, and enjoy an evening of live music under the open sky. The ambiance of these outdoor concerts is unparalleled, combining the natural beauty of Cape Cod with the power of live performances.

To plan your summer concert and performance experiences on Cape Cod, keep an eye on the event calendars of local venues, theaters, and community organizations. Check out the lineup of the Cape Cod Melody Tent, as well as the schedules for outdoor concerts in parks and town centers. Be sure to secure your tickets in advance for popular events, as they tend to sell out quickly.

So, as the sun sets on Cape Cod's picturesque landscapes, let the music and performances sweep you away into a world of enchantment and artistic expression. From lively concerts to captivating theatrical productions, the summer entertainment scene on Cape Cod promises to leave you with cherished memories and a deeper appreciation for the arts. Embrace the magic of live performances and let the music be the soundtrack to your summer adventures on Cape Cod.

Food and Wine Festivals

Prepare your taste buds for a delectable journey through Cape Cod's vibrant culinary scene. As summer arrives, so do the region's highly anticipated food and wine festivals, where renowned chefs, local artisans, and wine connoisseurs come together to celebrate the flavors of Cape Cod. From seafood delicacies to farm-to-table creations, these festivals offer a feast for both the senses and the soul.

Cape Cod's food and wine festivals showcase the region's rich culinary heritage, highlighting the abundance of fresh ingredients sourced from the surrounding waters and fertile farmlands. Step into a world brimming with tantalizing aromas, savory dishes, and perfectly paired wines as you embark on a gastronomic adventure like no other.

During these festivals, you'll have the opportunity to indulge in an array of culinary delights, each showcasing the skill and creativity of the talented chefs and artisans of Cape Cod. From elegant tasting menus to street food-inspired pop-ups, there is something to satisfy every palate. Sample succulent seafood specialties, savor farm-fresh produce, and treat yourself to decadent desserts that showcase the region's finest ingredients.

Accompanying the delectable food offerings, Cape Cod's food and wine festivals also showcase a diverse selection of wines, craft beers, and spirits. Raise a glass and discover new flavors as you explore wine tastings, cocktail seminars, and pairing sessions led by industry experts. From crisp whites to robust reds, and refreshing brews to artisanal cocktails, these festivals offer a comprehensive experience for both food and wine enthusiasts.

In addition to the culinary delights, food and wine festivals on Cape Cod often feature live entertainment, cooking demonstrations, culinary competitions, and educational workshops. Engage yourself in the vibrant atmosphere, interact with passionate chefs and artisans, and gain insights into the latest culinary trends and techniques. It's an opportunity to learn, be inspired, and connect with like-minded food lovers.

To plan your culinary adventure, keep an eye on the schedules and tickets for Cape Cod's food and wine festivals. Some of the most popular festivals include the Cape Cod Food and Wine Festival, the Wellfleet OysterFest, and the Provincetown Portuguese Festival. These events often span multiple days and take place at various locations across the Cape, giving you ample opportunities to indulge in the region's culinary delights.

Whether you're a food enthusiast, wine aficionado, or simply someone who appreciates the pleasures of the palate, Cape Cod's food and wine festivals are not to be missed. Indulge in the flavors of the Cape, discover new culinary experiences, and savor the finest offerings that the region has to offer. Let the food and wine festivals be your gateway to a world of taste, creativity, and culinary exploration on Cape Cod.

Art and Craft Fairs

Cape Cod is a haven for artists and craftsmen, and there's no better way to experience the region's vibrant arts scene than by attending one of its many art and craft fairs. These fairs bring together talented artisans, painters, sculptors, photographers, and creators of all kinds, offering visitors a unique opportunity to explore and purchase one-of-a-kind artworks and handcrafted treasures.

Throughout the year, Cape Cod hosts a variety of art and craft fairs that showcase the immense talent and creativity of the local artistic community. From quaint seaside villages to bustling town centers, these fairs transform outdoor spaces into open-air galleries where art enthusiasts can connect with artists directly, learn about their creative processes, and find that perfect piece to take home.

Strolling through the aisles of an art and craft fair, you'll be captivated by the diverse range of artwork on display. Admire stunning landscapes painted with vibrant brushstrokes, intricate sculptures that tell stories, captivating photographs that freeze moments in time, and handcrafted jewelry that reflects the beauty of Cape Cod's natural surroundings. Whether you're a seasoned art collector or simply appreciate the beauty of handmade craftsmanship, there's something for every taste and style at these fairs.

Beyond the visual feast, art and craft fairs often feature live demonstrations, workshops, and interactive experiences where visitors can engage with artists and learn about their techniques. Immerse yourself in the creative process, gain insights into the inspirations behind the artworks, and perhaps even try your hand at a new artistic endeavor. These fairs foster a sense of community, creativity, and appreciation for the arts.

Attending an art and craft fair on Cape Cod is not just about acquiring beautiful artwork; it's also an opportunity to support local artists and artisans who pour their hearts and souls into their creations. By purchasing artwork directly from the artists themselves, you can establish a personal connection and gain a deeper understanding of the stories and meanings behind each piece.

To discover the art and craft fairs happening on Cape Cod, keep an eye on local event listings, artist guild websites, and community bulletin boards. Some of the notable fairs include the Provincetown Art Association and Museum's Art in the Park, the Falmouth ArtMarket, and the Hyannis Village Green Art & Craft Show. These events often take place in picturesque outdoor settings, allowing you to soak up the beauty of Cape Cod while immersing yourself in its artistic offerings.

So, whether you're an art enthusiast, a collector, or simply someone who appreciates the beauty of handcrafted treasures, make sure to visit one of Cape Cod's art and craft fairs. Delve into a world of creativity, meet talented artists, and discover unique artworks that will add a touch of Cape Cod's artistic spirit to your life. Let these fairs be your window into the vibrant arts scene that thrives on the shores of Cape Cod.

Seasonal Celebrations

Cape Cod embraces the changing seasons with joy and enthusiasm, and throughout the year, the region comes alive with a variety of seasonal celebrations. From lively festivals to cherished traditions, these events showcase the unique character and spirit of Cape Cod, offering visitors a chance to embrace the local culture and create lasting memories.

No matter the time of year, there's always something to celebrate on Cape Cod. Each season brings its own charm and festivities, from the vibrant colors of spring to the warm glow of summer, the crisp air of fall, and the cozy ambiance of winter. Whether you're a local resident or a visitor, these seasonal celebrations provide a glimpse into the heart of Cape Cod's vibrant community.

In the spring, Cape Cod welcomes the blooming of flowers and the return of migratory birds with festivals such as the Cape Cod Daffodil Festival. Experience the beauty of thousands of daffodils in bloom, attend parades, and enjoy live music and entertainment. Spring also marks the start of the fishing season, and you can join in the excitement by attending events like the Blessing of the Fleet, where local fishing boats are blessed for a safe and bountiful season.

As summer arrives, Cape Cod truly comes alive with a plethora of events and celebrations. From Independence Day parades and fireworks to lively beach parties and concerts, there's no shortage of festivities to enjoy. Embrace the beach culture and join in the sandcastle contests, beach volleyball tournaments, and clam bakes that define summer on Cape Cod. Make sure to mark your calendar for the iconic Cape Cod Baseball League games, where you can witness talented college players compete in a quintessential American pastime.

As the leaves change color and the air becomes crisp, Cape Cod welcomes the fall season with open arms. Harvest festivals, apple picking, and pumpkin patches abound, providing opportunities to savor the flavors of the season. Explore the local farms and indulge in freshly pressed apple cider, warm apple pies, and vibrant fall foliage. Don't miss the Cape Cod Scallop Festival, a beloved event that celebrates the region's famous scallops with live music, arts and crafts, and, of course, plenty of delicious seafood.

Winter on Cape Cod is a time of cozy charm and holiday magic. Embrace the festive spirit by attending the lighting of the town Christmas trees, holiday parades, and local theater productions of beloved holiday classics. Take part in the Polar Plunge and start the new year with a refreshing dip in the frigid Atlantic Ocean. Don't forget to experience the enchantment of Cape Cod's picturesque towns adorned with twinkling lights and decorations.

To stay updated on the seasonal celebrations happening on Cape Cod, keep an eye on local event calendars, community websites, and tourism information. Whether you're in search of cultural experiences, family-friendly entertainment, or an opportunity to fully engage with local traditions, Cape

Cod's seasonal celebrations offer something for everyone.

So, no matter the time of year, be sure to join in the seasonal celebrations on Cape Cod. Embrace the unique festivities, connect with the community, and create cherished memories as you partake in the vibrant spirit of each season.

Practical Information

To make the most of your visit to Cape Cod, it's essential to have the necessary practical information at your fingertips. From important contact details to helpful tips and recommendations, this chapter provides you with all the essential information you need to navigate the region with ease and ensure a smooth and enjoyable trip.

Discover essential details about local transportation options, including getting to Cape Cod and navigating the region once you're here. Find guidance on selecting the perfect accommodation that suits your needs and preferences. Learn about packing essentials to ensure you're well-prepared for your Cape Cod getaway.

While Cape Cod offers a picturesque and inviting destination for travelers, it's important to prioritize safety during your visit. By following some basic safety guidelines, you can ensure a smooth and secure experience as you explore the region's natural beauty and engage in various activities.

1. **Sun Safety:**
   - Cape Cod's sunny beaches and outdoor activities call for adequate sun protection. Remember to apply sunscreen with a high SPF, wear a wide-brimmed hat, sunglasses, and protective clothing.
   - Seek shade during the peak hours of the day when the sun's rays are strongest, typically between 10 am and 4 pm.
   - Stay hydrated by drinking plenty of water, especially in the summer months when temperatures can be high.

2. **Water Safety:**
   - When enjoying Cape Cod's beautiful beaches, pay attention to the lifeguard instructions and adhere to posted signs and flags indicating water conditions.
   - Swim in designated areas and be mindful of currents and tides, which can change rapidly.
   - Keep an eye on children at all times while they are in or near the water.
   - If you're engaging in water activities like kayaking or boating, wear a life jacket and ensure you have the necessary safety equipment on board.

3. **Outdoor Adventure Precautions:**

- If you're planning on hiking or biking on Cape Cod's trails, stay on marked paths and trails to avoid getting lost or venturing into restricted areas.
- Carry a map, compass, or GPS device to help you navigate unfamiliar terrain.
- Let someone know about your planned outdoor activities and expected return time.
- Dress appropriately for outdoor adventures, considering weather conditions and wearing sturdy footwear.

4. **Wildlife Encounters:**
    - Cape Cod is home to various wildlife species, including seals, birds, and deer. Admire wildlife from a safe distance and avoid approaching or feeding them.
    - If you encounter marine wildlife such as seals while swimming or kayaking, maintain a respectful distance to avoid disturbing them.
    - When hiking or exploring nature preserves, be aware of your surroundings and take precautions in areas where wildlife may be present.

5. **Road Safety:**
    - Follow traffic laws and signs when driving on Cape Cod's roads. Be mindful of pedestrians and cyclists, especially in popular tourist areas.

- Use caution when crossing busy roads and intersections.
- Observe speed limits and adjust your driving speed to match road and weather conditions.

6. **Emergency Preparedness:**
    - Familiarize yourself with the location of emergency services, including hospitals, police stations, and fire stations, in case of any unforeseen circumstances.
    - Keep emergency contact numbers handy on your phone or in a readily accessible location.

By keeping these safety tips in mind, you can enjoy a safe and memorable experience on Cape Cod. Embrace the natural beauty and engaging activities while prioritizing your well-being and that of others around you.

Local Customs and Etiquette

When visiting Cape Cod, it's important to familiarize yourself with the local customs and etiquette to ensure a respectful and enjoyable experience. The region has a unique cultural identity and a strong sense of community, and by observing these customs, you can interact with locals in a positive and meaningful way.

1. **Friendliness and Politeness:**
    - Cape Codders are known for their warm and friendly nature. Greet people with a smile and a friendly "hello" or "good morning" when interacting with locals.

- Be courteous and polite in your interactions with service providers, such as waitstaff, hotel staff, and shopkeepers.

2. **Beach and Outdoor Etiquette:**
   - When visiting Cape Cod's beaches, be mindful of others by respecting their space and privacy.
   - Follow beach regulations and guidelines, including rules regarding alcohol, littering, and bonfires.
   - Dispose of trash properly and help keep the beaches clean and pristine.

3. **Conservation and Environment:**
   - Cape Cod takes pride in its natural beauty and preservation efforts. Respect the environment by refraining from littering, picking up after yourself, and disposing of waste in designated areas.
   - Avoid damaging or disturbing plant and animal life, including sand dunes, vegetation, and wildlife habitats.
   - Follow any specific guidelines or restrictions in protected areas or nature reserves.

4. **Driving and Traffic:**
   - Observe traffic rules and regulations while driving on Cape Cod's roads. Follow speed limits and be mindful of pedestrians and cyclists.

- Use turn signals when changing lanes or making turns, and yield to other drivers as necessary.
- Parking can be limited in popular areas, so be considerate when parking your vehicle, ensuring you're not blocking driveways or access points.

5. **Tipping and Service:**
   - In restaurants and bars, it is customary to leave a gratuity for good service. The standard tipping rate is generally 15-20% of the total bill.
   - Tip other service providers, such as taxi drivers, hotel staff, and tour guides, based on the quality of service received.

6. **Dress Code:**
   - Cape Cod has a relaxed and casual atmosphere, particularly in beach towns. Dress comfortably and casually for most occasions, unless a specific dress code is mentioned.
   - Pack appropriate clothing for the season and activities you plan to engage in, including beachwear, comfortable shoes, and layers for varying weather conditions.

7. **Respect for Local Traditions:**
   - Cape Cod has a rich maritime history and a strong connection to its fishing heritage. Show respect for local traditions and livelihoods, such as

fishing practices and the local seafood industry.
- Respect the privacy of residents and avoid trespassing on private property, especially in residential areas.

By understanding and embracing the local customs and etiquette of Cape Cod, you can deeply connect with the community and show respect for the region's unique culture. By demonstrating courtesy and consideration, you'll have a more enriching and authentic experience on your Cape Cod journey.

GPS Coordinates Index

Cape Cod is a diverse region with numerous attractions and points of interest spread across its various towns and villages. To assist you in navigating the area, this chapter provides a GPS coordinates index, which includes the latitude and longitude coordinates of key locations mentioned throughout the book. These coordinates can be used with a GPS device, smartphone app, or navigation system to help you find specific places with accuracy. Please note that the coordinates provided here are approximate and may vary slightly depending on the mapping service or device used. It's always a good idea to double-check the coordinates and confirm the accuracy before setting out on your journey.

1. **Cape Cod National Seashore:**
   - Coast Guard Beach: Latitude 41.8444, Longitude -69.93766
   - Marconi Beach: Latitude 41.8919, Longitude -69.9611

- Nauset Light Beach: Latitude 41.8586, Longitude -69.9515
- Race Point Beach: Latitude 42.0806, Longitude -70.2194
- Head of the Meadow Beach: Latitude 42.0545, Longitude -70.0831

2. **Lighthouses:**
   - Highland Light: Latitude 42.0395, Longitude -70.0621
   - Nauset Light: Latitude 41.8601, Longitude -69.9523
   - Chatham Light: Latitude 41.6714, Longitude -69.9498
   - Race Point Light: Latitude 42.0625, Longitude -70.2428
   - Stage Harbor Light: Latitude 41.6812, Longitude -69.9624

3. **Popular Towns and Villages:**
   - Provincetown: Latitude 42.0526, Longitude -70.1859
   - Chatham: Latitude 41.6821, Longitude -69.9597

Distance Reference Guide

To assist you in planning your travels around Cape Cod, Here's a distance reference chart for key destinations and attractions mentioned throughout the book. Please note that the distances provided are approximate and may vary depending on the specific routes and modes of transportation used.

1. **Distances between Major Towns and Villages:**

- Provincetown to Chatham: 35 miles (56.33 kilometers)
- Chatham to Falmouth: 41 miles (65.98 kilometers)
- Falmouth to Hyannis: 20 miles (32.19 kilometers)
- Hyannis to Wellfleet: 34 miles (54.72 kilometers)
- Wellfleet to Sandwich: 45 miles (72.42 kilometers)

2. **Distances between Popular Attractions and Towns:**
   - Cape Cod National Seashore to Provincetown: 15 mi (24.14 kilometers)
   - Highland Light to Chatham: 25 miles (40.23 kilometers)
   - Nauset Light to Wellfleet: 10 miles (16.09 kilometers)
   - Marconi Beach to Eastham: 10 miles (16.09 kilometers)

3. **Distances between Cape Cod and Nearby Destinations:**
   - Cape Cod to Martha's Vineyard: 53 miles (85.30 kilometers)
   - Cape Cod to Nantucket Island: 30 miles (48.28 kilometers)
   - Cape Cod to Plymouth: 32 miles (51.50 kilometers)
   - Cape Cod to Boston: 70 miles (112.65 kilometers)
   - Cape Cod to Provincetown: 48 miles (77.25 kilometers)

4. Distances between Airports and Cape Cod:
- Boston Logan International Airport to Cape Cod: 72 miles (115.87 kilometers)
- Barnstable Municipal Airport (Hyannis) to Provincetown: 47 miles (75.64 kilometers)

Please note that the distances provided are intended as a general reference and may vary based on the specific routes, traffic conditions, and mode of transportation chosen. It is always advisable to consult updated maps, GPS devices, or online mapping services for the most accurate and current distance information.

By referring to this distance reference guide, you can better plan your itinerary, estimate travel times, and make informed decisions while exploring Cape Cod.

CAPE COD TRAVEL GUIDE

Conclusion

As we come to the end of this Cape Cod Travel Guide, we hope that it has provided you with valuable information and insights to make your visit to Cape Cod a memorable and enjoyable experience.

Throughout the chapters, we have explored the natural beauty, rich history, and diverse attractions that this captivating region has to offer.

From the picturesque beaches and charming coastal towns to the fascinating lighthouses and breathtaking national seashore, Cape Cod truly has something for every traveler. Whether you're seeking outdoor adventures, cultural exploration, or simply relaxation by the seaside, Cape Cod delivers with its unique blend of natural wonders and cultural treasures.

We've covered the practical aspects of planning your trip, including the best time to visit, transportation options, accommodation choices, and essential items to pack. Additionally, we've provided detailed insights into the various regions, popular towns, must-see attractions, and outdoor activities that make Cape Cod a remarkable destination.

For those seeking historical and cultural experiences, we've highlighted the significant landmarks, museums, art galleries, and events that showcase the rich heritage and artistic traditions of Cape Cod. We've also included day trip suggestions to nearby islands and towns, allowing you to expand your exploration and discover more of this beautiful region.

During your adventure, we encourage you to fully embrace the local customs, savor the fresh seafood, and engage with the friendly residents who call Cape Cod home. The events and festivals will provide you with a glimpse into the vibrant community spirit and provide opportunities to create lasting memories.

Remember to respect the natural environment and follow safety guidelines while enjoying the outdoor adventures that Cape Cod offers. Keep in mind the practical information, emergency contacts, and local etiquette to ensure a smooth and memorable experience.

As you venture out and explore the scenic landscapes, picturesque towns, and hidden gems of Cape Cod, we hope that this travel guide has been a valuable companion, providing you with the necessary information to navigate and appreciate the wonders of this unique destination.

May your journey to Cape Cod be filled with unforgettable experiences, cherished moments, and a deep appreciation for the natural beauty and cultural heritage that make this region truly special. Happy travels!

Printed in Great Britain
by Amazon